# Death in September
## The Antietam Campaign

## CIVIL WAR CAMPAIGNS AND COMMANDERS SERIES

Under the General Editorship of Grady McWhiney

PUBLISHED

# Death in September
## The Antietam Campaign

Perry D. Jamieson

## McWhiney Foundation Press
### McMurry University
#### Abilene, Texas

*In memory of Adaline Jamieson*

**Cataloging-in-Publication Data**

Jamieson, Perry D.
    Death in September: the Antietam Campaign/ Perry D. Jamieson.
    p.  cm. — (Civil War campaigns and commanders)
    Includes bibliographical references and index.
    ISBN 1-893114-06-6

    1. Antietam, Battle of, Md., 1862. 2. Maryland Campaign,
1862.
    I. Title. II. Series
    E474.65.J35 1995
    973.7'336—dc20

                                                    95–5819
                                                       CIP

McMurry Station, Box 637
Abilene, TX  79697-0637

Printed in the United States of America

ISBN 1-893114-06-6
10 9 8 7 6 5 4 3

Book Designed by Rosenbohm Graphic Design

All inquiries regarding volume purchases of this book should be
addressed to McWhiney Foundation Press, McMurry Station, Box 637,
Abilene, TX  79697-0637.
Telephone inquiries may be made by calling (915) 793-4682

A NOTE ON THE SERIES

Few segments of America's past excite more interest than
Civil War battles and leaders. This ongoing series of brief,
lively, and authoritative books–*Civil War Campaigns and
Commanders*–salutes this passion with inexpensive and
accurate accounts that are readable in a sitting. Each volume,
separate and complete in itself, nevertheless conveys the
agony, glory, death, and wreckage that defined America's
greatest tragedy.

In this series, designed for Civil War enthusiasts as well as
the newly recruited, the emphasis is on telling good stories.
Photographs and biographical sketches enhance the narrative
of each book, and maps depict events as they happened. Sound
history is meshed with the dramatic in a format that is just
lengthy enough to inform and yet satisfy.

Grady McWhiney
Series Editor

We acknowledge the cooperation of the U.S. Army Military History Institute at Carlisle Barracks, Pennsylvania for the photographs of Abraham Lincoln, George B. McClellan, William B. Franklin, Stonewall Jackson, Lafayette McLaws, Jesse Reno, Joseph Hooker, John B. Hood, D.H. Hill, Robert Toombs, Joseph K.F. Mansfield, Alpheus S. Williams, Abner Doubleday, James Ricketts, Alexander R. Lawton, William E. Starke, Clarissa Barton, George S. Greene, Samuel W. Crawford, William H. French, Israel B. Richardson, Thomas F. Meagher, Robert Rodes, Francis C. Barlow, and Isaac P. Rodman.

We acknowledge the cooperation of The Library of Congress, Washington, D.C., for the photographs of Robert E. Lee, Ambrose E. Burnside, James Longstreet, A.P. Hill, George G. Meade, John Sedgwick, and John B. Gordon.

We are grateful to Mr. Jim Enos for his expert assistance.

# CONTENTS

# CAMPAIGNS AND COMMANDERS SERIES

## Map Key

### Geography

|  | Trees |
|--|-------|
|  | Marsh |
|  | Fields |
|  | Strategic Elevations |
|  | Rivers |
|  | Tactical Elevations |
| )( | Fords |
|  | Orchards |
| — — · — — | Political Boundaries |

### Human Construction

|  | Bridges |
|--|---------|
| ┼┼┼┼┼┼┼┼┼ | Railroads |
|  | Tactical Towns |
| ● | Strategic Towns |
| ▪ | Buildings |
| ▪ | Church |
| ✕ | Roads |

### Military

|  |  | Union Infantry |
|--|--|----------------|
|  |  | Confederate Infantry |
|  |  | Cavalry |
| ‖ı |  | Artillery |
|  |  | Headquarters |
| △ △△ △ △△ △ △ △ |  | Encampments |
| ⊐⊏ |  | Fortifications |
| ЛЛЛЛ |  | Permanant Works |
|  |  | Hasty Works |
|  |  | Obstructions |
| ✗ |  | Engagements |
|  |  | Warships |
|  |  | Gunboats |
|  |  | Casemate Ironclad |
|  |  | Monitor |
|  |  | Tactical Movements |
|  |  | Strategic Movements |

*Maps by*
***Donald S. Frazier, PhD.***
***Abilene, Texas***

# MAPS

# PHOTOGRAPHS

The brief biographies accompanying the photographs were written
by Grady McWhiney and David Coffey.

# Death in September
## The Antietam Campaign

# 1

## THE CONTESTANTS

Many years after the Civil War, Southerners draped General Robert E. Lee's soldiers in the golden mantle of the Lost Cause, making them into a nearly invincible legion. On September 4, 1862, when the Army of Northern Virginia began wading the Potomac River, the reality of the present sharply contrasted with the myth of the future. On that Thursday, Lee led a collection of dirty, ill clothed, hungry, and battle worn young men.

Marylanders were not impressed with the military bearing of the Southerners who marched through their villages and towns during September 1862. After the Civil War, a Shepherdstown woman who had spent four years watching both Federals and Confederates pass through her region candidly described the Rebel foot soldiers she saw that month. "When I say they were hungry," she recounted, "I convey no impression of the gaunt starvation that looked from their cavernous eyes.... There are always stragglers, of course, but never before or after did I see anything comparable to the demoralized state of the Confederates at this time." General Lee himself acknowledged the truth of the matter: "The army is not properly equipped for an invasion of an enemy's territory." Having fought a major battle at Manassas less than a week before, the Southerners moved directly into their next campaign. Their numbers were small, particularly in view of the ambitious operations they were about to undertake north of the Potomac. Although the exact strength of the Army of

## ROBERT E. LEE

Born Virginia 1807; son of Ann Hill (Carter) Lee and Henry "Light-Horse Harry" Lee, who died when Robert was eleven; received early education in Alexandria, Virginia, schools; graduated second in his class at U.S. Military Academy in 1829, without receiving a demerit in four years; appointed 2d lieutenant of engineers in 1829, 1st lieutenant in 1836, and captain in 1838; served at Fort Pulaski, Fort Monroe, Fort Hamilton, and superintended engineering project for St. Louis harbor; married Mary Ann Randolph Custis, whose father's estate of "Arlington" on the Virginia shore of the Potomac opposite Washington became Lee's home in 1857 after the death of his father-in-law; in 1846 Lee, then a captain, joined General Winfield Scott's Vera Cruz expedition and invasion of Mexico; Lee's extraordinary industry and capacity won him a brilliant reputation and the lasting confidence and esteem of Scott; wounded in 1847, Lee won three brevet promotions to major, lieutenant colonel, and colonel for gallant and meritorious conduct in the battles of Cerro Gordo, Contreras, Churubusco, and Chapultepec; served as superintendent of the U.S. Military

Northern Virginia when it entered Maryland probably never will be known, the largest estimates put it at 55,000 men.

For all their handicaps, these Southern troops carried great hopes on their shoulders as they entered the border state of Maryland. Ever since the beginning of the Civil War, they had consistently bested their opponents. The Confederates won the first of these victories on July 21, 1861, when the initial large operation of the Civil War ended in the First Battle of Manassas. Leading a Union army from Washington, D.C., Brigadier General Irvin McDowell got no further than a stream called Bull Run, fewer than thirty miles from the national capi-

Academy from 1852 to 1855; promoted to lieutenant colonel 2d Cavalry in 1855; commanded Marines sent to Harpers Ferry to capture John Brown after his raid; promoted to colonel 1st Cavalry in 1861; having refused command of Federal armies, his first Confederate command led to failure at Cheat Mountain in western Virginia; after serving along the South Atlantic coast, he returned to Virginia as military advisor to President Jefferson Davis until June 1862 when he replaced the wounded Joseph E. Johnston in command of forces that became known as the Army of Northern Virginia; for nearly three years, Lee's aggressive campaigns and effective defenses frustrated Union efforts to capture the Confederate capital; not until February 1865—two months before his surrender—did he become over-all commander of Confederate forces; after the war, he accepted the presidency of Washington College (later changed to Washington and Lee University) in Lexington, Virginia, where he remained until his death in 1870. Theodore Roosevelt proclaimed Lee "without exception the very greatest of all the great captains." "Lee possessed every virtue of other great commanders without their vices," announced an orator. "He was a foe without hate; a friend without treachery; a victor without oppression, and a victim without murmuring. He was a public officer without vices; a private citizen without reproach; a Christian without hypocrisy and a man without guile." Bold, modest, and heroic, Lee once confessed that if war were less terrible he would become too fond of it. His greatest biographer characterized him as "a simple gentleman."

tal. Here the Confederate forces of Generals P.G.T. Beauregard and Joseph E. Johnston defeated and routed the Federals.

After an autumn and winter of organizing and drilling, the second major campaign in the Eastern theater of the war took place during the following spring and summer. McDowell's successor, Major General George B. McClellan, abandoned the overland route to Richmond and in March 1862 moved his enormous Army of the Potomac by water transports from Alexandria, Virginia, to Fort Monroe. The popular young commander, touted by some as the "Young Napoleon," slowly advanced up the peninsula between the York and the James rivers and by late June had reached the outskirts of the Confederate capital. Here the Southerners, by now led by General Robert E. Lee, attacked McClellan and drove him back to Harrison's Landing on the James. The Army of the Potomac later returned by water to the Washington defenses.

While McClellan had been moving up the Virginia Peninsula, the Confederates triumphed in a third major campaign. With a series of splendid marches and battles, Major General Thomas Jonathan "Stonewall" Jackson overcame an ill-led collection of small Union commands in the Shenandoah Valley. President Abraham Lincoln then combined these defeated units into a new army, which he entrusted to Major General John Pope.

This boastful leader, like Irvin McDowell, marched into northern Virginia and eventually was reinforced from McClellan's Army of the Potomac. Pope tried to match wits with Lee in a campaign of maneuver and soon found himself in waters far over his head. The Virginian overwhelmed his Federal opponent with superior scouting, planning, marching, and fighting. On August 29 and 30, 1862, this campaign culminated in the Second Battle of Manassas and Lee inflicted a stinging defeat on a befuddled Pope. When the Union forces retreated to the Washington defenses, the Southerners had won their fourth consecutive major campaign in the East and

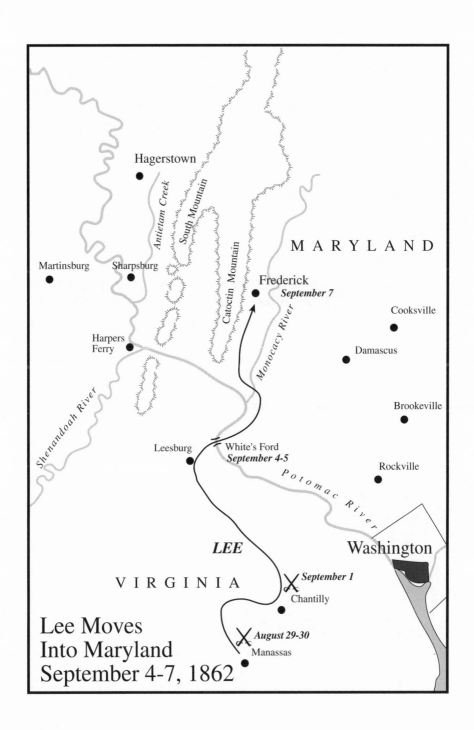

Hagerstown

Antietam Creek

South Mountain

Catoctin Mountain

MARYLAND

Martinsburg  Sharpsburg

Frederick
*September 7*

Cooksville

Damascus

Harpers
Ferry

Shenandoah River

Monocacy River

Leesburg

White's Ford
*September 4-5*

Brookeville

Rockville

Potomac River

LEE

Washington

VIRGINIA

*September 1*
Chantilly

Lee Moves
Into Maryland
September 4-7, 1862

*August 29-30*
Manassas

the way into Maryland and perhaps Pennsylvania stood open to them.

As General Lee led his soldiers across the Potomac, he held high expectations of what they might achieve during the weeks ahead. He hoped to shift the burdens of war from Virginia to Maryland, to gain support from the residents of that politically crucial border state, and to impress Great Britain and France with the Confederacy's military prowess and the likelihood of its ultimate triumph. And so, in spite of the Army of Northern Virginia's low supplies and shoddy appearance, its soldiers crossed the Potomac in high spirits. "The passage of the river by the troops marching in fours, well closed up," a

## ABRAHAM LINCOLN

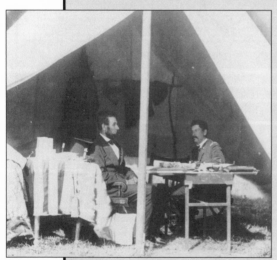

Born Kentucky 1809; received little formal education; family moved to Illinois where he held various clerking jobs; studied law; served in state legislature as a Whig; settled in Springfield, practiced law, and in 1842 married Mary Todd; retired from public life after one term in U.S. Congress, 1847–49; joined Republican party in 1856 and entered the growing debate over sectionalism; in 1858 beaten for U.S. Senate by Stephen A. Douglas, but emerged from their famous debate a national figure; nominated by Republicans and elected president in 1860; determined to preserve Union; issued Emancipation Proclamation after Union victory at Antietam in 1862; reelected in 1864; mortally wounded by John Wilkes Booth April 14, 1865; died the next day.

young staff officer recalled, "the laughing, shouting, and singing, as a brass band in front played 'Maryland, My Maryland,' was a memorable experience."

The army lost none of its confidence when the farmers and villagers of the border state failed to rally to the Stars and Bars. Lee's men made their way north, foraging along the way and enduring temperatures which stubbornly remained in the high seventies day after day. On September 7 the Southerners began camping comfortably around the prosperous little city of Frederick and their commander began pondering the next step in his campaign.

The reports that Lee had triumphed at Second Manassas and had crossed the Potomac spread alarm in the North. Faced with the defeat of Pope and the threat of invasion, President Lincoln made one of the most difficult decisions of his life. On September 2 he formally reappointed Major General George B. McClellan to lead the Army of the Potomac.

The commander in chief turned to this ambitious general in desperation, and not with confidence. McClellan already had failed once against Lee, only a few months before on the Peninsula, and in the process the egotistical Young Napoleon had antagonized President Lincoln, Secretary of War Edwin Stanton, and others. Furthermore, "Little Mac" was a partisan Democrat whose views on slavery and on the political objectives of the Northern war effort were at odds with those of the Republican administration he served. By reinstating McClellan, Lincoln had put himself in the position of Mexican War President James K. Polk, a Democrat whose theater generals, Zachary Taylor and Winfield Scott, had been Whigs. Above all else, the chief executive sought a military victory which would preserve the Union and he urgently wanted McClellan to defeat Lee. Yet as the leader of his political party and a first-term president, Lincoln hoped that his general would not win a victory that would make Little Mac a popular war hero who could oust his own commander in chief from the White House.

Despite all these hazards in the decision, the brooding head of state reappointed McClellan, largely because he seemed as good a choice as any of the generals then available near Washington. In late August and early September 1862 the national government faced a military crisis which might have been fatal to the Union. Lincoln desperately needed a commander who could rally the Federal troops in the Washington defenses after their defeat at Second Manassas and rapidly get

## GEORGE B. McCLELLAN

Born Pennsylvania 1826; attended preparatory schools in Philadelphia; entered University of Pennsylvania in 1840, but left upon appointment to the U.S. Military Academy in 1842, from which he graduated second in the class of 1846; brevetted 2d lieutenant of engineers 1846; promoted to 2d lieutenant 1847; participated in Mexican War as part of General Winfield Scott's command; brevetted 1st lieutenant 1847 for gallant conduct at the battles of Contreras and Churubusco and captain for gallantry at the battle of Chapultepec; following the war he served as instructor of engineering at West Point for three years; translated French regulations on bayonet exercise which the U.S. Army adopted in 1852; part of expedition to explore the sources of the Red River; promoted to 1st lieutenant in 1853; chief engineer on General Persifor F. Smith's staff; examined rivers and harbors in Texas; surveyed route for railroad across the Cascade Mountains; promoted to captain in the 1st Cavalry in 1855, but never joined his regiment; appointed member of a board of officers to study the European military systems; spent a year abroad, visiting most of the principal countries as well as the theatre of operations in the Crimea; McClellan's reports received high praise; in 1857 he resigned his army commission to become chief engineer of the Illinois Central

them into the field against the intimidating Robert E. Lee and his confident army. There was no time to bring in an officer from the war's Western theater and McClellan was readily at hand, residing only a few blocks from the War Department. Little Mac had two long suits: his popularity with the soldiers and his ability to organize an army, precisely the strengths the Union needed on September 2, 1862. President Lincoln knew that McClellan could restore the morale of the Army of the

Railroad; became vice president in charge of operations in Illinois in 1858; in 1860 he moved to Cincinnati to become president of the Ohio & Mississippi Railroad; with the outbreak of the Civil War, became major general Ohio Volunteers, commanding all state troops April 1861; less than a month later, President Abraham Lincoln appointed him major general U.S. Army in command of the Department of the Ohio; led campaign into western Virginia where he was victorious at Rich Mountain July 1861; following General Irvin McDowell's defeat at First Bull Run, McClellan was selected to lead the Army of the Potomac; appointed general-in-chief of the Armies of the United States upon the retirement of General Scott November 1861; zealously worked to improve the army's organization and training; devoted himself to the reconstruction of the Army of the Potomac; his spring 1862 Peninsular Campaign ended in failure after coming within miles of Richmond; superseded as general-in-chief by General Henry Halleck; after General John Pope led the newly designated Army of Virginia to defeat at Second Bull Run, McClellan was recalled and the Army of the Potomac regained its place as the primary Eastern force; during the Maryland Campaign September 1862, he stopped General R.E. Lee's northern advance at Antietam but failed to use his superior force to advantage; failed to aggressively pursue Lee; much displeased, Lincoln removed him from command and he saw no further duty; Democratic presidential candidate opposing Lincoln 1864; after war he worked as an engineer and served as governor of New Jersey, 1878-81; died 1885; General McClellan's efforts in organizing and training the Army of the Potomac were his chief contributions. However his seeming unwillingness to damage his creation and a general lack of aggressiveness prevented his ultimate success.

Potomac and rebuild its units more effectively than any other available officer. "There is no man in the Army," the president declared, "who can man these fortifications and lick these troops of ours into shape half as well as he.... If he can't fight himself, he excels in making others ready to fight."

**McClellan on horseback**

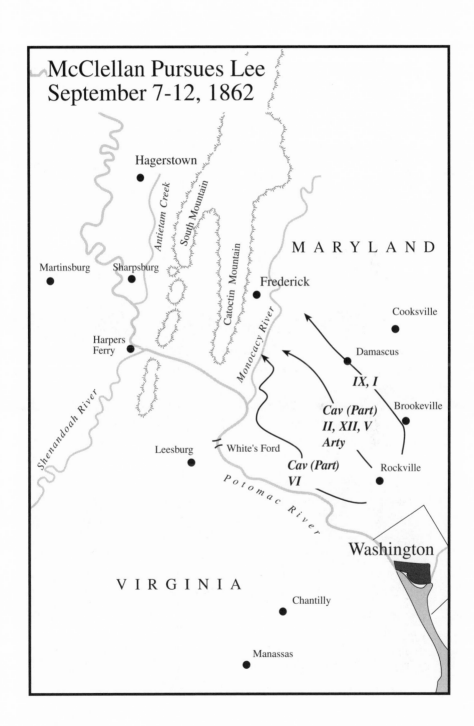

# McClellan Pursues Lee
# September 7-12, 1862

Hagerstown

Antietam Creek

South Mountain

Catoctin Mountain

M A R Y L A N D

Martinsburg    Sharpsburg

Frederick

Cooksville

Monocacy River

Harpers
Ferry

Damascus

IX, I

Shenandoah River

Brookeville

Cav (Part)
II, XII, V
Arty

Leesburg    White's Ford

Rockville

Cav (Part)
VI

Potomac River

Washington

V I R G I N I A

Chantilly

Manassas

McClellan rapidly met Lincoln's initial hopes. He established his headquarters at Rockville, outside of Washington, and began organizing the Army of the Potomac for the crucial campaign ahead. The Union soldiers, roughly 85,000 of them, greeted their commander as a returning hero. The Young Napoleon cantered through their camps on his dashing black horse, "Daniel Webster," and twirled his cap to their cheers. Just as the president had hoped, McClellan quickly revived the Army of the Potomac. Within four days he had rallied the Union troops and had them on the roads leaving Washington, in pursuit of Lee.

Under other circumstances McClellan, a meticulous administrator, probably would have taken weeks or months to pre-

## AMBROSE EVERETT BURNSIDE

Born Indiana 1824; apprenticed to a tailor and worked in a shop until friends of his father, an Indiana legislator, secured him an appointment to the U.S. Military Academy, where he graduated eighteenth in the class of 1847; appointed 2d lieutenant in 3rd Artillery in 1847, but saw little service in Mexico; promoted to 1st lieutenant in 1851; married Mary Richmond Bishop of Rhode Island in 1852 and resigned from army a year later to manufacture a breech-loading rifle he invented; company went bankrupt in 1857; major general in the Rhode Island militia and treasurer of the Illinois Central Railroad before the Civil War; in 1861 organized and became colonel of 1st Rhode Island Infantry, which was among the earliest regiments to reach Washington; became friend of President Lincoln and received promotion to brigadier general of volunteers in August 1861 after commanding a brigade at the Battle of Bull Run; in 1862 commanded a successful operation

pare the Army of the Potomac for an autumn campaign, but the Confederate invasion of Maryland had denied him that luxury. Little Mac had to shake the knots out of his forces and reorganize them while they were on the march. He fanned out his army in three great columns, which eventually would converge on Frederick. The right wing, the First and the Ninth Corps, moved toward that city by way of the hamlet of Brookeville. This force, commanded by McClellan's friend Major General Ambrose E. Burnside, could drive north to intercept Lee, should the Confederates swing toward Baltimore. The left wing, the Sixth Corps and two unattached divisions, moved out into Maryland along the north bank of the Potomac. Major General William B. Franklin, a cautious com-

along the North Carolina Coast; commissioned a major general of volunteers and received awards and thanks from various states; at Sharpsburg he wasted too much time crossing Antietam Creek and attacking the Confederate right; after twice declining command of the Army of the Potomac, he finally accepted, although he considered himself incompetent and proved himself correct by crossing the Rappahannock River in December 1862 and making a disastrous attack on the awaiting Confederate army at Fredericksburg; "I ought to retire to private life," Burnside informed President Lincoln, who after relieving him of command in the East assigned him to command the Department of the Ohio; at Lincoln's urging, he advanced into East Tennessee and in November 1863 repulsed an assault on Knoxville by Confederates under James Longstreet; Burnside and his Ninth Corps returned to the East in 1864 to serve under Grant from the Wilderness to Petersburg; blamed by General George Meade for the Union failure at the Crater, Burnside shortly thereafter went on leave and never returned to duty; in 1865 he resigned his commission; after the war he became president of various railroad and other companies; elected governor of Rhode Island in 1866 and reelected in 1867 and 1868; elected to U.S. Senate from Rhode Island in 1874, where he served until his death at Bristol, Rhode Island, in 1881.

## WILLIAM B. FRANKLIN

Born Pennsylvania 1823; graduated U.S. Military Academy 1843, first in his class of forty-three that included U.S. Grant; brevetted 2d lieutenant assigned to engineers; part of Great Lakes survey team 1843–45; with  Philip Kearney's Rocky Mountain expedition 1846; won two brevets for Mexican War service, including one for gallantry at Buena Vista; from 1848 to 1861 he was involved in numerous engineering projects, among these was the construction of a new dome for the national capitol; taught engineering at West Point; gained slow but steady promotion reaching captain in 1857; at the outbreak of the Civil War he was commissioned colonel of the 12th U.S. Infantry and brigadier general U.S. Volunteers shortly thereafter; commanded a brigade at First Bull Run and a division in the Washington defenses following that debacle; commanded a division and then the Sixth Corps during the Peninsular Campaign; promoted to major general U.S. Volunteers July 1862; directed the Sixth Corps during the Maryland Campaign and was conspicuously involved at Crampton's Gap, South Mountain, and Antietam, September 1862; commanded the Left Grand Division at Fredericksburg, after which he was accused by General Ambrose Burnside of failing to follow orders; although not disciplined, his career was irreparably damaged; sent West, he commanded the Nineteenth Corps in General N.P. Banks's Red River Expedition during which he was twice wounded, ending his field service; brevetted brigadier general U.S. Army for his actions in the Peninsular Campaign and major general U.S. Army for war service, he was retired in 1866; from then until 1888, he was an executive with Colt's Firearms Manufacturing Company; he also supervised the construction of the Connecticut state capitol and held a variety of public offices until his death at Hartford in 1903. Although he owned a relatively solid service record, General Franklin could not overcome the stigma of the disaster at Fredericksburg.

mander like McClellan, would keep these units alert to the possibility that the Confederates might return south and turn the Federal left flank. The army's center, the Second and Twelfth Corps led by the aggressive ex-dragoon Major General Edwin V. Sumner, took the direct route to Frederick, largely following the old National Road.

The Young Napoleon had rallied and reorganized the Army of the Potomac rapidly but when it came to marching, he remained the same old McClellan. From Washington to Frederick, his soldiers covered an average of only six miles a day. Small groups of bluecoats stopped to play cards along the roadsides, or to enjoy the cool drinks offered them by well-meaning local citizens. On September 12 the lead units of the army entered Frederick and found that the Confederates had left the area two days ahead of them.

# 2

# A Daring Plan

At Frederick, Lee had made his first vital decision since leaving Virginia. He would shift his line of communications west to the Shenandoah Valley, securing this route by capturing the 11,000 Federals who garrisoned Harpers Ferry. Lee decided to seize this Union depot for another reason as well: it held a tempting collection of small arms, artillery, wagons, and other supplies which the Army of Northern Virginia sorely needed.

On September 9 Lee issued Special Orders 191, which detailed his plan for capturing Harpers Ferry. Taking one wing of the Army of Northern Virginia, the daring Stonewall Jackson would encircle the Union garrison. The number of Confederates sent against Harpers Ferry, like Lee's total strength, is not known but it is certain that it far exceeded the Union command at this crucial depot. While this operation was

## JAMES LONGSTREET

Born South Carolina 1821; graduated U.S. Military Academy fifty-fourth in his class in 1842; appointed a brevet 2d lieutenant in the 4th Infantry the same year; promoted to 2d lieutenant in the 8th Infantry in 1845, and to 1st lieutenant in 1847; won brevet promotions to captain and major for gallant conduct in the battles of Contreras, Churubusco, and Molino del Rey during the Mexican War; served as regimental adjutant from 1847 to 1849; promoted to captain in 1852 and to major (paymaster department) in 1858; appointed Confederate brigadier general, served at First Manassas, and promoted to major general in 1861; distinguished service during Peninsular Campaign, Second Manassas, Sharpsburg, and Fredericksburg in 1862; promoted to lieutenant general in 1862, "Old Pete" became General Lee's senior corps commander; on detached service south of the James River in May 1863 thus missing the action at Chancellorsville; commanded right wing of Lee's army at Gettysburg in July 1863; took his corps by rail to Chickamauga, Georgia, in September 1863 to help defeat General William S. Rosecrans, but failed in his

attempt to capture Knoxville, Tennessee; returned to Virginia in 1864 in time to participate in the Battle of the Wilderness, where he sustained a critical wound that incapacitated him until late fall; led his corps during closing months of the war in defense of Richmond; surrendered with Lee to Grant at Appomattox Court House; after the war, he settled in New Orleans, became a Republican, and as a state militia officer led black troops against Confederate veterans during Reconstruction disturbances; enjoyed political patronage from Republicans; wrote his war memoirs, *From Manassas to Appomattox*; died at Gainesville, Georgia, in 1904. Lee called Longstreet "my old War Horse." An able battlefield tactician, he was at times stubborn, quarrelsome, and overconfident in his ability as an independent commander.

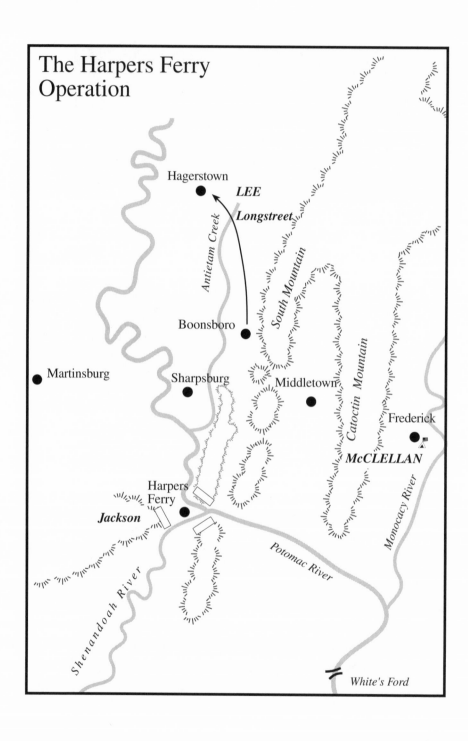

The Harpers Ferry
Operation

underway, Lee would accompany his other chief subordinate, Major General James Longstreet, another hard-fighting combat officer, through Boonsboro to Hagerstown. Jackson would reduce Harpers Ferry, reunite his command with the main body of the army, and, enriched by their booty from the captured depot, the Southerners would continue their campaign.

The danger for the Confederates in this bold plan was that the Army of the Potomac heavily outnumbered the separated wings of Lee's army. If McClellan pursued rapidly and pushed his forces between Jackson and Longstreet, the Confederacy would be in peril. Lee believed that this eventuality was unlikely and that the supplies at Harpers Ferry were well worth the gamble. He had every confidence in General Jackson's ability to operate on his own, given Stonewall's successes as an independent commander in the Shenandoah Valley and Second Manassas campaigns. Moreover, Lee doubted McClellan would move rapidly enough to threaten either Confederate wing. The day before the Southern commander issued Special Orders 191, he told one of his subordinates that his opponent was "an able general but a very cautious one.... His army is in a very demoralized and chaotic condition, will not be prepared for offensive operations—or he will not think it so—for three or four weeks." Supremely optimistic, Lee allotted three days to complete the Harpers Ferry operation.

Lee was correct in his assessment that McClellan was cautious, but in this campaign the Young Napoleon also was fortunate beyond belief. While chatting with visitors at his headquarters in Frederick on September 13, Little Mac was handed a document that represented one of the greatest intelligence coups in American military history. Earlier that morning the 27th Indiana had camped in a meadow on the outskirts of town, an area the Southerners had left just ahead of the Federals. While resting with Sergeant John M. Bloss, Corporal Barton W. Mitchell spotted a bulky envelope lying in the grass: it contained three cigars wrapped in a copy of Special Orders

191. The Confederates had made a horrible error, one which has never been fully explained. Someone, perhaps a courier galloping across the field, had dropped a copy of Lee's campaign plan on this campground, carelessly leaving it for the Yankees to find. The two noncoms promptly took the document to their company captain. He and other officers rapidly passed it up the chain of command, and before noon, McClellan had in front of him, as he soon reported to President Lincoln, "all the plans of the Rebels."

For decades, Civil War veterans and historians explained what the Northern commander *should* have done next.

## THOMAS J. JACKSON

Born Virginia 1824; graduated seventeenth of fifty-nine cadets in his 1846 class at the U. S. Military Academy; appointed 2d lieutenant in 3rd Artillery; participated in War with Mexico in 1847; brevetted captain for gallantry at Contreras and Churubusco and major for his conduct at Chapultepec; resigned from the U.S. Army in 1852 to accept a professorship of artillery tactics and optics at the Virginia Military Institute in Lexington, where he enforced rigid discipline, expelled several cadets, and won the hatred of many others; students called him, behind his back: "Tom Fool," "Old Blue Light," "crazy as damnation," and "the worst teach that God ever made." Jackson's first wife, Elinor Junkin, died in childbirth; a later marriage to Mary Anna Morrison produced a daughter. In 1861 Jackson joined the Confederate army; appointed colonel and then brigadier general, he won his famous nickname "Stonewall" in July at the Battle of Manassas, where General Barnard E. Bee, observing the steadiness of Jackson's Virginians, shouted to his South Carolinians: "Look, men! There stands Jackson like a stonewall!

McClellan should immediately, the afternoon of the thirteenth, have pushed his army west as rapidly as possible, through the gaps of South Mountain and between the widely divided and hopelessly outnumbered wings of Lee's tired army. But Little Mac moved as he always had: slowly. He remained idle the afternoon and evening of the thirteenth, waiting until after darkness fell to order an advance west "at daybreak in the morning." From the time McClellan was handed the incredible gift of Lee's "Lost Order" until the first Federal began marching toward South Mountain, about eighteen hours passed. While the clocks in Frederick ticked ahead, the Union cause missed

Rally behind the Virginians!" Promoted to major general, Jackson began in March 1862 his brilliant Shenandoah Valley Campaign; in June he shifted his army to assist Lee in the Seven Days' Battle near Richmond; in August he fought Federal forces at Cedar Mountain, Groveton, and Second Manassas; in September, during Lee's Maryland Campaign, he captured a large Union garrison at Harpers Ferry and then rejoined Lee's army for the Battle of Sharpsburg; promoted in October to lieutenant general and commanding half of Lee's forces, Jackson repulsed a major Federal assault in December at Fredericksburg. In May 1863 Jackson fought his last battle at Chancellorsville, where he made a spectacular flanking attack on the exposed Federal right flank and then rode out to locate the enemy's position; while returning in the darkness, he was mistaken for Federal cavalry and shot by his own troops. Jackson developed pneumonia and dies on May 10, 1863. "I know not how to replace him," lamented Lee. "Without disparagement to others, it may be safely said he has become, in the estimation of the Confederacy, emphatically 'the hero of the war.' Around him clustered with peculiar warmth their gratitude, their affections, and their hopes," reported Secretary of War James A. Seddon. "Stonewall Jackson," as his most recent biographer observed, "ranks among the most brilliant commanders in American history. Even though his field service in the Civil War lasted but two years, his movements continued to be studied at every major military academy in the world."

an opportunity which, for all its men and wealth, it could never regain. "You can ask me for anything you like," Napoleon once told a subordinate, "except time."

South Mountain lay between McClellan at Frederick and Lee's dangerously divided army. Small numbers of soldiers could hike over the range at any point, but an army of 85,000 men, with their wagons, tents, artillery, ambulances, black-smithing equipment, and other encumbrances, could cross it only by marching through Turner's, Fox's, or Crampton's Gaps. These three passes through South Mountain now became the crucial terrain of the Maryland campaign. While McClellan

## LAFAYETTE McLAWS

Born Georgia 1821; graduated from the U.S. Military Academy, where he ranked forty-eighth among fifty-six graduates in the class of 1842; appointed brevet 2d lieutenant 6th Infantry 1842; 2d lieutenant 7th Infantry 1844; lst lieutenant 1847; captain 1851; served at various frontier posts; joined his uncle General Zachary Taylor to partici-pate in the War with Mexico only to be transferred to General Winfield Scott's army at Vera Cruz, where McLaws became ill and returned home; in 1849 he married Emily Allison Taylor, a niece of General Taylor's; following the Mexican War, McLaws made the rounds of frontier posts until Georgia seceded in 1861; elected colonel of the 10th Georgia Infantry, McLaws took his new com-mand to Virginia where he gained promotion to brigadier general; in 1862, he saw action at Yorktown before being promoted to major general in May; he fought at Antietam in September and

squandered time, Southern units took up the defense of these important gaps. Lee ordered Major General Daniel Harvey Hill, Stonewall Jackson's brother-in-law, to hold his division in the northernmost passes, Turner's and Fox's, about a mile apart, and other Confederate commands marched to reinforce him. Major General Lafayette McLaws, a bushy-bearded Georgian, diverted some of his division from the Harpers Ferry operation to defend Crampton's Gap, about five miles south of the other two. Unless the Confederates made a stand at South Mountain, the Army of Northern Virginia faced a calamity.

defended Marye's Heights at Fredericksburg in December; his lack of initiative at Salem Church in May 1863 upset General Lee, and McLaws failed to receive either of the promotions to corps command in the Army of Northern Virginia following the death of Stonewall Jackson; at Gettysburg, McLaws became so incensed with Longstreet that he called him. "a humbug, a man of small capacity, very obstinate, not at all chivalrous, exceedingly conceited, and totally selfish." Transferred along with Longstreet to the West, McLaws found himself relieved of command during the Knoxville Campaign; when McLaws pressed for a court-martial, Longstreet charged him with improper preparations for an attack at Knoxville; the court's findings and its subsequent disapproval by President Davis produced "a vindication of McLaws and a humiliation of Longstreet." Sent to Georgia to defend Savannah, McLaws surrendered with Johnston's army after failing to halt Sherman's advance. Unable to make a living after the war, McLaws confessed: "I am without means, having lost all." He died July 22, 1897, in Savannah, Georgia. Douglas S. Freeman emphasized McLaws's "bad luck." He dragged along "on the road to Sharpsburg," noted Freeman; at Chancellorsville, he had "a chance to deliver a hammerstroke," but he hesitated; ultimately, McLaws had "no luster in the red glare of Gettysburg, though the fault is scarcely his."

# 3

# SOUTH MOUNTAIN
# AND HARPERS FERRY

On September 14 McClellan belatedly moved to gain the passes of South Mountain. Major General Jesse Reno, the army commander's West Point classmate, led the Ninth Corps against Fox's Gap, while on his right another two-star general, the handsome and popular Joseph Hooker, brought the First Corps up the steeply winding road into Turner's Gap. About six miles to the south, General Franklin assaulted Crampton's Gap.

A sharply contested series of engagements followed. The Confederates who defended South Mountain were not entrenched, but they held strong positions. Their attackers had to climb steep hillsides and make their way through ravines and the Southerners also enjoyed the cover of woods, fences, and stone walls. The Federal advantage in numbers mounted during the day, but the Rebels waged a determined defense in the face of the lengthening odds.

At Fox's Gap, Brigadier General Samuel Garland ignored the advice of one of his colonels that he move to a safer position and was mortally wounded on the firing line of his North Carolina brigade. Later in the battle General Reno met the same fate, shot from his saddle in front of his corps. Brigadier General John Gibbon's Black Hat Brigade, sporting the high-crowned Hardee hat worn in the Regular Army before the Civil

## JESSE RENO

Born (West) Virginia 1823; graduated U.S. Military Academy 1846, eighth in his class of fifty-nine that included George B. McClellan, Stonewall Jackson, and George E. Pickett; brevetted 2d lieutenant assigned to ordnance; won two brevets in Mexican War; taught mathematics at West Point 1849; served on numerous surveys and ordnance boards; 1st lieutenant 1853; chief of ordnance on Colonel Albert Sidney Johnston's Utah Expedition 1857–59; commanded Mount Vernon (Alabama) Arsenal 1859–61; until its seizure by Confederates; captain 1860; commanded arsenal at Fort Leavenworth, Kansas, 1861; brigadier general U.S. Volunteers November 1861; led brigade in General Ambrose Burnside's Carolina expedition December 1861–April 1862; commanded division in Federal District of North Carolina; major general U.S. Volunteers July 1862; joined General John Pope's Army of Virginia, ably directing Burnside's Ninth Corps at Second Bull Run and Chantilly; during the action at South  Mountain September 14, 1862, General Reno was mortally wounded while directing the Ninth Corps advance. A competent officer, Reno was sorely missed in the subsequent Battle of Antietam. Reno, Nevada, was named in his honor.

## JOSEPH HOOKER

Born Massachusetts 1814; graduated U.S. Military Academy 1837, twenty-ninth in his class of fifty cadets; brevetted 2d lieutenant assigned to artillery; on frontier duty, fought in Seminole wars, and held a staff assignment at West Point; served conspicuously in Mexican War, earning three brevets; captain 1848; resigned his commission 1853; engaged in farming in California and served as colonel in the state militia; offered his services to the Union at the outbreak of the Civil War but was initially snubbed owing to poor relations with General Winfield Scott; commissioned brigadier general U.S. Volunteers May 1861; led a division in the

Peninsular Campaign and at Second Bull Run; major general U.S. Volunteers May 1862; commanded First Corps and was wounded at Antietam September 1862; promoted brigadier general U.S. Army to date from the battle; named to command the Army of the Potomac January 1863; routed by badly outnumbered Confederates at Chancellorsville, but received the thanks of Congress for his subsequent defense of Washington May 1863; relieved at his own request in June; sent West, took command of the newly formed Twentieth Corps Army of the Cumberland, which he led with great success at Chattanooga and during the Atlanta Campaign; resigned when overlooked for the command of the Army of the Tennessee following the death of General James B. McPherson; for the balance of the war he exercised various departmental commands; brevetted major general U.S. Army for Chattanooga victory; remained in the regular army until his retirement in 1868; died 1879. Although the disaster at Chancellorsville tainted his career, General Hooker proved to be a competent combat officer at division and corps level. While he hated his sobriquet "Fighting Joe," it was nonetheless appropriate.

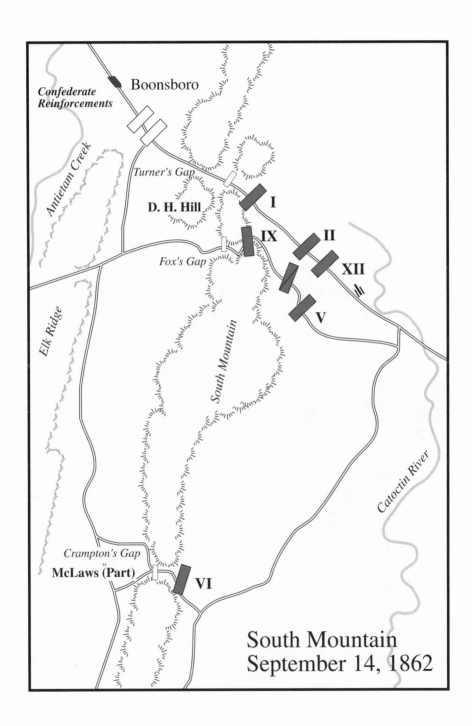

Confederate Reinforcements

Boonsboro

Antietam Creek

Turner's Gap

D. H. Hill

I

IX

II

Fox's Gap

XII

V

Elk Ridge

South Mountain

Catoctin River

Crampton's Gap

McLaws (Part)

VI

South Mountain
September 14, 1862

War, made its way into Turner's Gap as the day's fighting came to an end. A story later became popular that McClellan had watched this advance and remarked that the unit "must be made of iron," although in fact Gibbon's brigade was not called the Iron Brigade until after South Mountain—and other brigades claimed the same nickname. The Federals lost about 2,300 total casualties in this stoutly fought battle and the Confederates 3,200.

The Southern defenders made a determined stand, but the Federals were tenacious, too, and the dead weight of numbers eventually told in their favor. In the middle of the night of September 14–15, the last exhausted Confederates abandoned

## AMBROSE POWELL HILL

Born Virginia 1825; graduated fifteenth in the class of 1847 at the U.S. Military Academy; 2d lieutenant 1st Artillery in 1847 and served in Mexico, but saw no action; 1st lieutenant in 1851; participated in Florida Seminole campaigns; served in D.C. office of coast survey, 1855 to 1860; married Kitty Morgan McClung, sister of John Hunt Morgan, in 1859; resigned from U.S. Army in 1861; appointed colonel of 13th Virginia Infantry; in 1862 promoted to brigadier general; commanded brigade and won praise at Williamsburg; promoted to major general and given command of the Confederacy's largest division, which he led successfully but with heavy losses during the Battle of the Seven Days; transferred after a disagreement with Longstreet to Stonewall Jackson's command, Hill received praise for his actions at Cedar Mountain and Second Manassas, yet enjoyed his greatest fame for saving the Army of Northern Virginia from defeat by his timely arrival on Lee's right flank at Sharpsburg; in December

South Mountain and retreated into the Antietam valley, where Lee hoped to reunite his army. With the sunrise, McClellan's corps began moving freely through the gaps in the range.

The Southerners who fought at South Mountain achieved a great deal by their stubborn defense of its crucial passes, buying the time their comrades needed to complete the capture of Harpers Ferry. Stonewall Jackson had directed the Confederate forces which had skillfully converged on this Union depot from three directions. Harpers Ferry stands at the confluence of the Shenandoah and Potomac rivers and is dominated on all sides by high ground. By dusk of September 14, the Southerners had the garrison encircled and their artillery

1862 his actions at Fredericksburg heightened a controversy between Hill and Jackson that ended only with Stonewall's death following the Battle of Chancellorsville in May 1863; promoted to lieutenant general and given command of the newly formed Third Corps in Lee's army, Hill opened the Battle of Gettysburg, but sickness limited his effectiveness; he repulsed Federals at Falling Waters, Maryland, on the retreat to Virginia, but suffered his worst defeat making a bold attack at Bristoe Station in October; in 1864 he fought in the Wilderness, but illness deprived him of command from May 8-21; participated in actions from the North Anna River to Cold Harbor, and in Lee's defense of Petersburg, where from June 1864 to March 1865 Hill met and defeated "every Federal effort to break Lee's right"; late in March he took sick-leave, his best biographer explains, suffering from kidney malfunctions that slowly produced uremia, the results of a gonorrhea infection contracted during a summer 1844 furlough from West Point; Hill returned to the front on April 2, 1865, where he was killed trying to reestablish his lines. Genial but quarrelsome, reckless and impetuous in battle, only five feet nine inches tall, and weighing just 145 pounds, "Little Powell" favored bright red shirts and enjoyed the confidence of his troops. "A more brilliant, useful soldier and chivalrous gentleman never adorned the Confederate army," said General William Mahone.

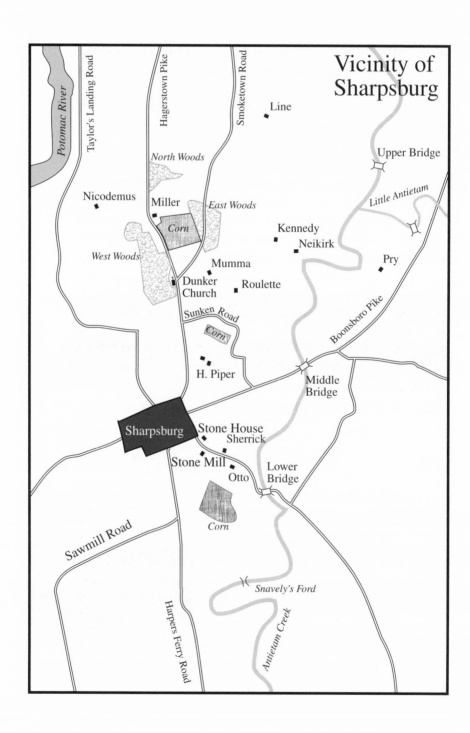

# Vicinity of Sharpsburg

## GEORGE GORDON MEADE

Born Spain of U.S. parents 1815; graduated from U.S. Military Academy 1835, nineteenth in his class; 2d lieutenant 3rd Artillery 1835; resigned in 1836 to become a civil engineer; re-entered army in 1842 as 2d lieutenant topographical engineers; brevet lst lieutenant 1846 for gallant conduct during Mexican War; lst lieutenant 1851; captain 1856; brigadier general volunteers 1861; advanced from command of a brigade during the Seven Days (wounded at White Oak Swamp) and Second Bull Run to command of a division at Antietam and Fredericksburg, to command of the Fifth Corps at Chancellorsville; brigadier general U.S. Army 1863; selected by

President Lincoln to replace Joseph Hooker as commander of Army of the Potomac rather than the more qualified John F. Reynolds because Meade's foreign birth disqualified him from the presidency; showed remarkable courage in accepting battle at Gettysburg only two days after assuming army command; major general 1864; received thanks of Congress in 1864 for his contributions to Union victory; from the Wilderness to Appomattox, Meade was in the awkward posi-tion of commanding the Army of the Potomac while Grant, the overall commander, traveled with Meade's army; battle strain combined with this difficult command sit-uation helped make Meade so unpopular and quarrelsome that Grant seri-ously considered replacing him; a staff officer said of Meade: "I don't know any thin old gentleman with a hooked nose and cold blue eye, who, when he is wrathy, exercises less of Christian charity than my well-beloved Chief." Grant pronounced Meade "brave and conscientious, ...[a man who] commanded the respect of all who knew him." After the war, he commanded first the Division of the Atlantic and then Reconstruction Military District No. 3 (comprising Alabama, Georgia, and Florida); bitterly disappointed at not being appointed lieutenant general when Sherman replaced Grant as army commander, Meade returned to command the Division of the Atlantic; died of pneumonia in 1872, never having fully recovered from his White Oak Swamp wound.

## JOHN BELL HOOD

Born Kentucky 1831; graduated U.S. Military Academy 1853, forty-fourth in class of fifty-two that included Philip Sheridan, James B. McPherson, and John M. Schofield; commissioned 2d lieutenant; served on frontier most notably with the 2d Cavalry, a regiment that included R.E. Lee, A.S. Johnston, W.J. Hardee, G.H. Thomas, and many other future Civil War generals; resigned commission 1861 as 1st lieutenant; entered Confederate service, where he rose rapidly from lieutenant to colonel; commanded 4th Texas Infantry; brigadier general March 1862; commanded Texas Brigade, Army of Northern Virginia; major general October 1862; fought conspicuously at Gaines' Mill, Second Manassas, and Sharpsburg; led division at Fredericksburg and Gettysburg, where a wound rendered his left arm virtually useless; went West with Longstreet's Corps; wounded again, losing right leg, at Chickamauga; promoted lieutenant general September 1863; joined Army of Tennessee March 1864; commanded corps during Atlanta Campaign until chosen to replace J.E. Johnston in July 1864 with temporary rank of full general; fought series of battles around Atlanta; evacuated that city September 1, 1864; led army into Tennessee; fought bloody battle at Franklin in November; routed at Nashville in December; relieved at his own request January 1865; surrendered at Natchez, Mississippi, May 1865; after war engaged in business in New Orleans; married and fathered eleven children; died with wife and eldest daughter in yellow fever epidemic 1879. His memoir, *Advance and Retreat,* published posthumously. As a combat commander, Hood was unsurpassed. He ranks among the best brigade and division commanders in the war. While not ideally suited to corps or army command, he performed credibly during the Atlanta Campaign, but the utter failure of his Tennessee Campaign ended his military service and severely tarnished an otherwise stellar career.

in place on the heights which commanded the village. At day-break the next morning Jackson began a cannonade and the Northern commander, Colonel Dixon S. Miles, soon realized that resistance was useless. By 8 A.M. white flags began appearing among the Federal lines. The hapless Colonel Miles was mortally wounded by the artillery fire, leaving it to another Union officer to surrender the garrison. In addition to their prisoners, the Confederates gained more than 70 cannon, 13,000 small arms, 200 wagons, and other much needed supplies.

The Rebel defense of South Mountain also allowed Lee to begin pulling together his dangerously divided forces. About seventeen miles north of Harpers Ferry, Generals Longstreet and D.H. Hill began assembling their commands on the rolling ground near the village of Sharpsburg, just west of the Antietam Creek. Having captured the garrison at the Shenandoah and Potomac rivers, Stonewall Jackson marched north to join them. He left behind him at Harpers Ferry the temperamental Major General Ambrose Powell Hill and his division to parole the Union prisoners, load the newly-won weapons and supplies onto wagons, and later bring them to Lee.

The terms of the parole at Harpers Ferry were consistent with the rules of war recognized at the time. The Federals who surrendered were allowed to go free, after they took an oath not to fight again until a formal exchange of prisoners was arranged. When nineteenth-century soldiers gave their word to accept a parole, they usually honored their pledge. Their captors took their weapons, while allowing the officers to keep their sidearms and personal belongings and the men to retain their equipment. A parole offered a Civil War soldier an honorable deferment from combat and doubtless many of the Harpers Ferry Federals were happy to be excused from the ongoing campaign against Lee's veterans.

Historians have wondered why the Confederate commander, given his low numbers and dangerous situation, decided to face McClellan's masses, rather than retreat into Virginia. One prominent scholar of the Army of Northern Virginia has argued that standing at Sharpsburg was probably Lee's worst decision of the war. In his official reports to President Davis, the general himself offered no explanation, leaving the question open to speculation. Lee was a bold and aggressive leader, not inclined to break off a campaign until his opponent forced him to retreat. He may have fought at Sharpsburg in the hopes that counter-chances would develop for him during the combat. Lee knew that McClellan was a cautious man and dur-

## DANIEL HARVEY HILL

Born South Carolina 1821; graduated twenty-eighth of fifty-six at the U.S. Military Academy in 1842; appointed brevet 2d lieutenant 1st Artillery 1842; transferred to 3rd Artillery 1843; promoted to 2d lieutenant 4th Artillery 1845; 1st lieutenant 1847; served in Mexican War, brevetted captain for gallant conduct at Contreras and Churubusco, and brevetted major for meritorious conduct at Chapultepec; resigned from US Army 1849; professor of mathematics, Washington College, Virginia, 1848–54, Davidson College, North Carolina, 1854–59; he became superintendent of the North Carolina Military Institute at Charlotte from 1859 until the Civil War; elected colonel of the 1st North Carolina Infantry, which in June 1861 he led successfully at Big Bethel, Virginia; promoted to brigadier general, served in North Carolina, and returned to Virginia in 1862 as a major general; fought at Williamsburg, Seven Pines, and won praise from General R.E. Lee for his actions during the Seven Days; appointed commander of Department of North Carolina, but returned to division command in the Army of Northern Virginia shortly after Second Manassas; falsely accused of losing the

ing the Battle of Antietam and afterward, the Confederate general looked for opportunities to seize the initiative from his opponent.

Tuesday, September 16, proved to be one of the most perilous days in the history of the Army of Northern Virginia. Lee deployed his still-gathering divisions into a battle line west of the Antietam, knowing that even after all of his units reassembled they would remain small in comparison to the 85,000 Federals advancing toward him from the passes of South Mountain. Once again, McClellan's leisurely style of operation

Confederate battle plan in Maryland, he fought aggressively at Sharpsburg; poor health and failure to receive promotion to lieutenant general embittered Hill; he returned to administrative duties in North Carolina until in 1863 he accepted corps command in Braxton Bragg's Army of Tennessee; participated in combat at Chickamauga in September; engaged in bitter quarrel with Bragg in which President Davis favored Bragg and relieved Hill from command. Hill spent the rest of the war trying to clear his record, but could obtain only minor commands; in 1864 served as volunteer aide to General Beauregard; for a few days he commanded a division against Union General David Hunter at Lynchburg, Virginia; in 1865 Hill ended his military career by commanding the District of Georgia, fighting at Bentonville, North Carolina, and surrendering with General Johnston at Durham Station. After the war Hill published *The Land We Love,* a monthly magazine, 1866–69, and *The Southern Home,* during the 1870s; he also wrote a number of articles for Century Company's *Battles and Leaders of the Civil War;* in 1877 he became president of what would become the University of Arkansas; in 1885 he became president of Middle Georgia Military and Agricultural College; he resigned in 1889, dying of cancer in Charlotte on September 24. Contemporaries recognized Hill's "well deserved reputation as a hard fighter," but labelled him "harsh, abrupt, often insulting"—a man who would "offend many and conciliate none." He never resolved his quarrel with Davis and Bragg.

helped his opponent. The Federal leader spent the day study-
ing the positions of his own troops and of the Confederates
west of the Antietam, and mulling over his plans for the great
battle to come. On September 16, McClellan might have delivered a massive blow against the Army of Northern Virginia
before it was reunited and ready for battle. Instead, he con-
tented himself with probing the northern, or left, end of Lee's
line. As the evening approached, Brigadier General George
Gordon Meade, who later would win the critical Union victory
at Gettysburg, led his division against that of Brigadier
General John Bell Hood, one of the most aggressive of the
Southern commanders. A sharp fight took place in a woodlot
which was later named the East Woods. The Rebels checked
this belated and limited Federal advance, which served only to
warn Lee that McClellan probably intended to attack the
Confederate left flank the next morning.

Lee's staff pitched their headquarters tents in a woodlot at
the western edge of Sharpsburg, but they rarely found their
leader there on Wednesday, September 17, the day of the
Battle of Antietam. The commander of the Army of Northern
Virginia spent most of the hours of combat at the front with his
officers and men, exerting a strong, direct influence on the
course of the fighting. Early in the battle Lee rode to the
Confederate left flank and saw to the artillery dispositions
there. Later he and General D.H. Hill made their way along the
center, where the army commander encouraged the colonels
whose regiments held this part of the line. As the sun dropped
in the west, Lee was at the southern end of the battlefield,
where his soldiers fought the final action of the day.

In contrast to Lee, McClellan tried to direct his troops from
a distance. The Union commander made his headquarters in
the substantial two story red-brick residence of the prosperous
Philip Pry, more than half a mile east of the Antietam, and
rarely ventured far from it during the battle. His staff set up
telescopes on the farmyard lawn and, using a trapdoor to gain

access, on the farmhouse roof. Once the combat began, the black powder from scores of cannon and thousands of small arms filled the Antietam valley with clouds of white smoke and it is extremely doubtful that McClellan saw much of the battle, other than distant troop formations and their flags.

# 4

## POISED FOR ACTION

By the dawn of September 17 nearly all of Lee's divisions had gathered on what was to become the Antietam battlefield. The terrain offered some advantages to an army fighting a defensive battle. Antietam Creek ran between Lee's position and most of McClellan's army and many of the advancing Federals would have to cross this stream by fords or bridges. The attackers would also encounter extremely rolling terrain, woodlots, and fences. The topography at the Confederate center, an eroded farm lane known as the "Sunken Road," and on their right, the high ground overlooking the Lower Bridge across the Antietam, particularly favored the defenders. The area harbored only one serious drawback for Lee: if the attackers broke through his main lines, the Potomac would deny his artillery and wagons any quick escape.

On that Wednesday morning in mid-September, the

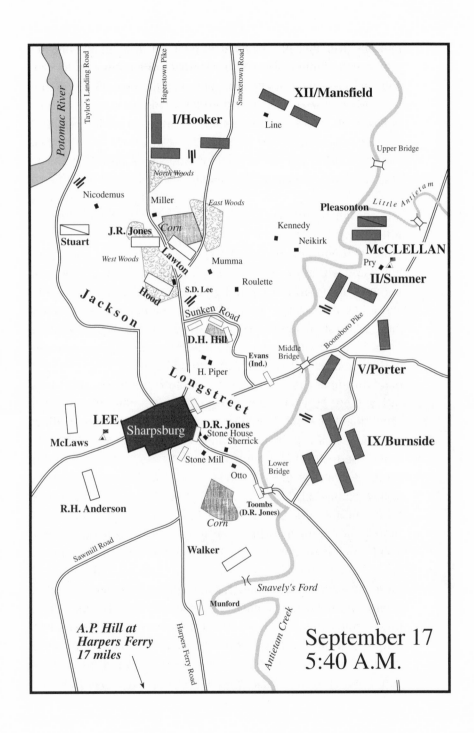

## ROBERT A. TOOMBS

Born Georgia 1818; attended University of Georgia; graduated Union College (New York) 1828; practiced law but soon became a prominent planter and politician, serving in the Georgia legislature and both houses of the U.S. Congress; delegate to the Montgomery Convention to establish a Confederate government; narrowly lost the vote for president that went to Jefferson Davis; disappointed, Toombs accepted the position of secretary of state; resigned to become brigadier general in the Provisional Army of the Confederate States of America July 1861; given command of the Georgia Brigade in what became the Army of Northern Virginia; led brigade in Peninsular Campaign and at Second Manassas; wounded during his brigade's defense of "Burnside's Bridge" at Sharpsburg (Antietam) September 1862; when he failed to receive the promotion he felt due, he resigned March 1863; became a vocal critic of the Davis administration; defeated in a bid for the Confederate Senate 1864; named adjutant and inspector general Georgia Militia; ineffectively led state troops in opposition to General W.T. Sherman's march through Georgia; barely escaped capture; fled to Cuba and then to Europe; returned to Georgia 1867; rebuilt his law practice and once again became influential in state politics, although he could not hold public office after refusing to seek a pardon; he continued to oppose the ideas of reconstruction until his death in 1885. General Toombs was highly critical of professional soldiers and West Point pedigrees. At one time he challenged his superior officer, General D.H. Hill, to a duel—Hill refused to give Toombs satisfaction. A true political general, Toombs was not without military ability.

Confederates held a great semicircle roughly four and a half miles long. The northern end of the line was near one of the bends in the Potomac River and the southern one fell along the Antietam Creek below Snavely's Ford. The dashing Major General J. E. B. Stuart used his cavalrymen to cover Lee's left flank, near the great river, and he deployed his horse artillery on the high ground of Nicodemus Hill. Stonewall Jackson held the front from Stuart's right to the Confederate center, where D.H. Hill's Division occupied the zigzagging Sunken Road. James Longstreet commanded the army's right, a line which ran in front of the village of Sharpsburg and included the Georgia brigade of Brigadier General Robert Toombs, a political rival of President Jefferson Davis, who had thrown forward two of his regiments to block the Yankees from exploiting the Lower Bridge across the Antietam. South of this crossing, an infantry division under Brigadier General John G. Walker of Missouri watched the lower fords of the creek, while a cavalry brigade led by Colonel Thomas T. Munford of Virginia patrolled the army's right flank.

When the battle opened on the morning of the seventeenth, four of Lee's divisions were not at the front. Hood, having skirmished with Meade the previous evening, rested his men behind the Dunker Church. The divisions of the capable Major General Richard H. Anderson and Lafayette McLaws arrived at Sharpsburg after sunrise, worn out by their marches during the campaign. That morning these exhausted soldiers lay resting in the fields near the village. Most significantly, A.P. Hill was still completing his tasks at Harpers Ferry.

Lee's lines at Sharpsburg were stretched pathetically thin. Thousands of his foot soldiers had dropped out of the ranks during the hot September march through Maryland. The long hikes, which became more strenuous when it became necessary to concentrate the dangerously divided army, took their toll. Many of the Southerners wore very poor shoes, or none at all, and hundreds of these men lay along the roadsides with hideous blisters while their regiments moved on. Others ate green corn, or whatever else they could forage, and suffered bouts of diarrhea. "We were hungry," one Rebel private sadly recalled, "for six days not a morsel of bread or meat had gone in our stomachs—and our *menu* consisted of apples and corn. We toasted, we burned, we stewed, we boiled, we roasted these two together, and singly, until there was not a man whose form had not caved in, and who had not had a bad

## JOSEPH KING FENNO MANSFIELD

Born Connecticut 1803; graduated U.S. Military Academy 1822, second in his class of forty; brevetted 2d lieutenant of engineers; engaged in constructing coastal defenses; 1st lieutenant 1832; captain 1838; chief engineer to General Zachary Taylor in Mexican War; brevetted through colonel for actions at Fort Brown, Monterey, where he was wounded, and Buena Vista; upon the recommendation of Secretary of War Jefferson Davis, named inspector general U.S. Army with the staff rank of colonel 1853; promoted brigadier general U.S. Army at the outbreak of the Civil War and given command of the Department of Washington, in which he directed the construction of the city's defenses; on duty at Fortress Monroe; participated in the actions against Norfolk and Suffolk, Virginia; commissioned major general U.S. Volunteers May 1862; named to command Twelfth Corps Army of the Potomac, he joined his new command just days before the Battle of Antietam; during that battle, September 17, 1862, General Mansfield was mortally wounded soon after his corps became engaged; he died the following day. While among the war's oldest field commanders, he was recognized as a fine officer and model of bravery in battle.

attack of diarrhoea." These hardships on the march, and the casualties at South Mountain, drained the Army of Northern Virginia. Lee's exact numbers at Sharpsburg probably never will be known; it is likely he fought the battle with 45,000 or fewer men.

Though McClellan had given the outnumbered Rebels ample time to entrench, the Confederate soldiers built no field works on the Sharpsburg battlefield. Lee's defense instead rested on the advantage that the range and accuracy of the rifled musket gave to all Civil War defenders, on the resolution of the Southern veterans, on the commander's ability to shift troops along his interior lines, and on some help from the battlefield's terrain. While the Federals would have to cross the Antietam and move through continually rolling ground to make their attacks, the Confederates would enjoy the cover of woods and rock outcroppings. Two Southern units in particular held positions that were naturally strong: D.H. Hill's Division in the Sunken Road, and Robert Toombs's regiments on the high ground overlooking the Lower Bridge.

Lee's soldiers faced a daunting host of Federals, stretched around a great arc from the Hagerstown Pike to the Lower Bridge. "Fighting Joe" Hooker's First Corps held the Union right and to its left camped the Twelfth Corps, led by Major General Joseph K. F. Mansfield, whose beard and head had turned white during his long years of service in the Old Army. South of these units and east of the Antietam lay the cavalry division of Brigadier General Alfred Pleasonton, a native of the District of Columbia; the Second Corps of General Edwin Sumner; and the Fifth Corps, which McClellan's friend Major General Fitz John Porter had assembled during the march through Maryland. The Ninth Corps held the army's left flank, at the far end of the line from the First Corps.

This deployment of the Ninth and First Corps dismantled the army's original organization, in which these two units had served together as one wing, under General Burnside.

McClellan apparently believed this arrangement had served its purpose during the pursuit through Maryland, but was now unnecessary. Generals Sumner and Burnside each were reduced from commanding two corps to one, a demotion which offended the commander of the right wing. Burnside persisted in the presumption that the First Corps had been detached from him only temporarily and that he remained a wing commander, while Brigadier General Jacob D. Cox of Ohio led the Ninth Corps. The mutton-chopped general's insistence on his own interpretation of the army's organization added another layer to the chain of command, soured his relations with McClellan, and delayed operations on the Union left flank.

McClellan's deployment for the battle also was flawed by the assignment of General Pleasonton's cavalry division to the Union center. Little Mac may have been thinking in terms of Napoleonic grand tactics, in which a massive mounted charge against the middle of the enemy's line might decide a battle, but he would have been wiser to have used his horsemen as Robert E. Lee did, to cover his flanks. The Federals particularly needed cavalrymen patrolling the roads beyond their left, toward Harpers Ferry. McClellan knew that the Confederates had captured that supply depot and his long experience as a soldier, and common sense, should have told him that a residual Southern force must be there still, paroling the prisoners and confiscating the booty. The Union commander should have assigned some of his troopers to watch the routes toward the south and to alert him if any Confederates approached from Harpers Ferry.

By the morning of September 17 McClellan had deployed most of the Army of the Potomac along the Antietam and, like Lee, still had additional troops which would join his main body during the battle. Leaving his camps around Rohrersville at dawn, General Franklin marched two divisions of the Sixth Corps into the rear of the Union forces, the lead unit arriving at about 10 A.M. and the other about an hour behind it. Major

General Darius N. Couch plodded his lone division of the Fourth Corps to the field from Maryland Heights, not reaching McClellan's lines until the morning after the battle. Brigadier General Andrew A. Humphreys, making a much greater effort, brought a third division of the Fifth Corps to join its comrades before 10 A.M. the same day.

# 5

# PLANS FOR BATTLE

Although McClellan believed Lee outnumbered him, he put aside some of his usual caution and brought himself to fight the Battle of Antietam on the offensive. The Young Napoleon knew that the Confederates were fighting with their backs to the Potomac. The river ran low that autumn, but nonetheless would pose a dangerous obstacle to a defeated army of tens of thousands, with its wounded, wagons, artillery, and other encumbrances. Little Mac may have hoped that a few blows by his army would throw back the Southerners, drive them in confusion into the coils of the Potomac, and inflict a defeat that might end the war.

Lee's aggressive mind-set contrasted sharply with McClellan's cautious one. The Southern commander fought on the defensive at Sharpsburg only because, heavily outnumbered and still gathering his army, he was forced to do so.

Even then, Lee conceded the initiative grudgingly and during the day-long battle he made division-sized counterattacks, exhausted all of his reserves, and looked for opportunities to seize the offensive. While the Federals were driving in his center along the Sunken Road, the Southern commander considered an attack against McClellan's right. The battle in fact ended with a Confederate offensive, A.P. Hill's timely thrust into the left flank of the Ninth Corps. Even after his army took its ghastly losses and had its brush with disaster at Sharpsburg, Lee's aggressive spirit remained undaunted. Just four days after the bloodbath at Antietam, he told President Davis: "...it is still my desire to threaten a passage into Maryland, to occupy the enemy on this frontier, and, if my purpose cannot be accomplished, to draw them into the [Shenandoah] Valley, where I can attack them to advantage." Few generals in American history, faced with Lee's circumstances on September 21, 1862, would have written such a dispatch.

As for McClellan's plans for the Battle of Antietam, he failed to communicate them clearly, to either his subordinates or posterity. Little Mac's three versions of his intentions for the engagement, two official reports and his memoirs, vary slightly among themselves. The earliest of his accounts, written about a month after the battle, probably gives the best indication of what was in his mind on the evening of September 16. In this preliminary report, McClellan explained that he intended to attack Lee's left and right and then, "as soon as one or both of the flank movements were fully successful, to attack their center with any reserve I might then have on hand." The attack against the Confederate left would be made by the corps of Hooker and Mansfield, the only ones west of the Antietam at dawn on the seventeenth. The attack on Lee's right would be made by Burnside's Ninth Corps, the sole one in position to do so.

What was McClellan's understanding of the role of these

two attacks and their relationship to each other?  Were they both to be main efforts, or was one secondary to the other? Little Mac's first report gave a muddled answer to these questions, suggesting that the commander's plan was not as clear

## ALPHEUS S. WILLIAMS

Born Connecticut 1810; graduated Yale University; studied law and travelled extensively before establishing a law practice in Detroit; served as a volunteer officer in the Mexican War; brigadier general of Michigan state troops; at the onset of the Civil War received a commission to brigadier general U.S. Volunteers May 1861; led a division under General N.P. Banks

in the Shenandoah Valley and at Cedar Mountain; commanded a division in the Second Corps Army of Virginia but not actively engaged at Second Bull Run;  directed the First Division of the newly formed Twelfth Corps and saw heavy fighting at Antietam, temporarily heading the corps following the death J.K.F. Mansfield; ably led his division at Chancellorsville and Twelfth Corps at Gettysburg; sent West with the Eleventh and Twelfth Corps, not actively engaged at Chattanooga; when the Eleventh and Twelfth Corps were merged into the Twentieth Corps, Williams received the First Division; led his division, and frequently the corps throughout the Atlanta Campaign, General W.T. Sherman's "March to the Sea," and through the Carolinas; brevetted major general U.S. Volunteers for war service, he mustered out of the volunteer organization 1866; minister to El Salvador 1866–69; unsuccessfully ran for governor of Michigan 1870; elected to U.S. House of Representatives 1874 and re-elected 1876; died in office 1878. General Williams was among the most solid of non-professional or "political" generals. Although he frequently commanded a corps, he was apparently never considered for permanent corps command. He ended the war a very experienced brigadier and deserving of higher rank.

in his own mind as it should have been. "The design," McClellan wrote, "was to make the main attack on the enemy's left—at least to create a diversion in favor of the main attack, with the hope of something more by assailing the enemy's right...." Lee's lines were so thin that hard blows, delivered simultaneously, at two or more points almost certainly would have carried the day. McClellan's confused explanation of his "design" for the attack gave no inkling of his enemy's tenuous situation or of his own sparkling opportunity.

Worse still, the Union commander failed to communicate his plans clearly to the officers he relied on to execute them. McClellan should have called his corps commanders to the Pry house on the evening of the sixteenth and explained in detail to them what he expected their units to achieve. The army leader convened no such conference and his failure to do so contributed to the slow and disjointed Union operations during the battle. A council of war was particularly needed, given McClellan's decision to direct the combat from long distance, spending his time at the Pry house rather than with his corps commanders and their subordinates.

The soldiers of both armies spent a miserable night, certain of battle in the morning. Thousands of young men slept fitfully or not at all, kept awake by an autumn rain, erratic picket fire, the odd noises of a rural night, and their persisting anxieties about the combat which approached first by the hour, then by the minute. Brigadier General Alpheus S. Williams, a division commander in the Twelfth Corps, described the night as "so dark, so obscure, so mysterious, so uncertain; with the occasional volleys of pickets and outposts, the low, solemn sound of the command as troops came into position, and withal so sleepy that there was a half-dreamy sensation about it all; but with a certain impression that the morrow was to be great with the future fate of our country. So much responsibility, so much intense, future anxiety!"

# 6

## HOOKER'S ATTACK

A soft and foggy dawn arrived at about 5:40 A.M., and as it became light enough for the anxious pickets to persuade themselves they could discern individual figures, their rifle fire increased with a nervous tempo. The skirmish lines lay quite close together at some places on the rolling terrain, especially at the northern end of the battlefield, where Meade had sparred with Hood the previous evening and where the main battle would begin this morning. As the daylight increased, artillerymen of both armies sighted their cannon and pulled their lanyards. The big Union guns along the eastern bank of the Antietam and some of those of the First Corps dueled against Colonel S.D. Lee's battalion at the Confederate center, Major John Pelham's horse artillery on Nicodemus Hill, and several of Stonewall Jackson's batteries. The Antietam valley rapidly filled with enormous billows of white smoke.

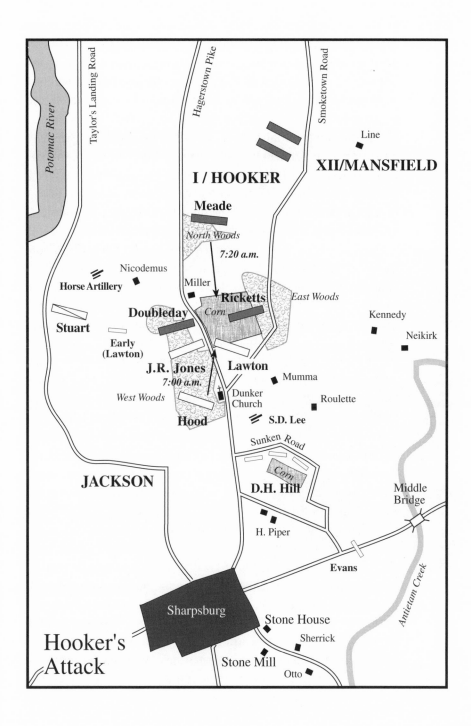

Hooker's
Attack

General Hooker opened the Battle of Antietam with a head-long attack, which began at about 6 A.M. Leaving one of his brigades in reserve, Brigadier General Abner Doubleday sent his three others south along the Hagerstown Pike toward the

## ABNER DOUBLEDAY

Born New York 1819; graduated U.S. Military Academy 1842, twenty-fourth in his class of fifty-six that included G.W. Smith, A.P. Stewart, D.H. Hill, R.H. Anderson, Lafayette McLaws, Earl Van Dorn, and James Longstreet; brevetted 2d lieutenant and assigned to artillery; served in Seminole wars and in Mexico; 1st lieutenant 1847; promoted to captain, reportedly directed the first shots fired in response to the Confederate bombardment of Fort Sumter 1861; following surrender of that post, served briefly in the Shenandoah Valley; commissioned brigadier general U.S. Volunteers January 1862; led a brigade at Second Bull Run; commanded a division at South Mountain, Antietam, and Fredericksburg; major general U.S. Volunteers November 1862; led division in First Corps at Chancellorsville; assumed direction of the corps following the death of General John F. Reynolds on the first day at Gettysburg; lacking confidence in Doubleday, General George G. Meade quickly replaced him with General John Newton; he saw no further field service during the war; brevetted through major general U.S. Army; in post-war army restructuring, became colonel 35th Infantry 1867; retired 1873; authored *Reminiscences of Forts Sumter and Moultrie* (1876) and *Chancellorsville and Gettysburg* (1882); died 1893; his brothers, Thomas and Ulysses, were also Federal officers. Despite his thirty years of service, General Doubleday is more recognized for his supposed invention of baseball than for his military career.

Dunker Church. Farther left, Brigadier General James Ricketts led his division into the East Woods. While one brigade of Meade's Pennsylvanians fought near Ricketts, the remaining two at first stood as the First Corps reserve and then they, too,

## JAMES RICKETTS

Born New York 1817; graduated U.S. Military Academy 1839, sixteenth in his class of thirty-one; brevetted 2d lieutenant 1st Artillery; on frontier and garrison duty; fought in Seminole wars; 1st lieutenant 1846; received no brevets for his Mexican War service; captain 1852; commanded a battery at First Bull Run, where he was severely wounded and fell into enemy hands; exchanged January 1862; promoted brigadier general U.S. Volunteers to date from August 1861 (First Bull Run); returned to duty May 1862; commanded a division at Cedar Mountain and 2d Bull Run; directed Second Division, First Corps, Army of the Potomac at South Mountain and Antietam September 1862; wounded at the latter, he was confined to administrative duty, including the court martial of General Fitz John Porter; returning to the field May 1864, led a Sixth Corps division in General U.S. Grant's Overland Campaign and at Petersburg; sent with Sixth Corps to Washington to oppose General Jubal Early's advance on that city; participated in General Philip Sheridan's Shenandoah Valley Campaign fall 1864; while in temporary command of the Sixth Corps at Cedar Creek he received yet another wound; returned to active duty only days before the surrender at Appomattox; brevetted through major general in both regular and volunteer ranks; continuing in the regular army he was retired from active duty for disability caused by wounds 1867, but continued to serve on courts martial until 1869; died at Washington 1887. General Ricketts sustained a total of six wounds during the war, the last of these left him disabled for the rest of his life.

## ALEXANDER ROBERT LAWTON

Born South Carolina 1818, to a distinguished local family; graduated thirteenth in a class of thirty-one at the U.S. Military Academy in 1839; appointed 2d lieutenant in 1st Artillery 1839; resigned 1840; graduated Harvard Law School 1842; practiced law in Savannah, Ga.; in 1849 became president of the Augusta & Savannah Railroad; served in Georgia legislature, 1855–56, and then in the state senate, 1859–60; at the Civil War's outbreak, Lawton became colonel of the 1st Georgia Infantry, which cap-

tured Fort Pulaski on January 3, 1861, before Georgia actually seceded; his early actions won Lawton promotion to brigadier general; early in 1862 he took command of a brigade of Georgia infantry attached to General Stonewall Jackson's command in the Shenandoah Valley; Lawton and his brigade participated with distinction during the Seven Days' Battle, as division commander, substituting for the wounded Richard Ewell; Lawton played a prominent part in the actions at Antietam, taking a serious wound; disabled for many months, he never entered active field service again; President Davis appointed him quartermaster general, but the Confederate Congress, feuding with Davis, refused to confirm the appointment; finally, after months of controversy, Lawton was confirmed; he performed his quartermaster duties capably to the war's end under two secretaries of war; in 1865 Lawton was one of the last officials to leave Richmond; briefly he joined Lee's retreating army; then traveled with the fleeing government until May 4 when Secretary of War John C. Breckinridge disbanded the War Department; Lawton returned to politics and his law practice after the war winning a seat in the Georgia legislature in 1870; he became state constitutional convention president in 1877, and a state delegate to Democratic conventions in 1880 and 1884; confirmed in 1887 as minister to Austria, he died in 1896 while visiting in New York and was returned to Savannah for burial. Lawton's biographer calls him "an able division commander," who "gave satisfaction wherever he served."

soon joined the fray.

Hooker's assault fell heavily on two divisions of Stonewall Jackson's Corps, commanded by Brigadier Generals Alexander R. Lawton and John R. Jones. Major Pelham's gunners contributed to the defense, too, throwing shells from Nicodemus Hill into the advancing blue ranks. By their fight with Meade's division in the East Woods, Hood's men had earned a rest behind the Confederate front but the battle was scarcely an hour old when Lawton called on them for help. Leaving their breakfast campfires in disgust, Hood's Rebels launched an angry counter-attack from the West Woods. Jackson also received assistance from another quarter. D.H. Hill, who held the Confederate center with five brigades, sent three of them to aid Stonewall's men.

## WILLIAM E. STARKE

Born Virginia 1814; successful cotton broker in Mobile and New Orleans; returned to Virginia at the onset of the Civil War; aide-de-camp to General Robert S. Garnett during that general's ill-fated western Virginia campaign; appointed colonel 60th Virginia Infantry; the brigade served in various commands before joining General A.P. Hill's Division in the Seven Days' Battles June 1862; promoted brigadier general August 1862; led brigade in General Stonewall Jackson's Corps Army of Northern Virginia during Second Manassas Campaign and assumed command of the Stonewall Division following the wounding of General W. B. Taliaferro; led his brigade in the capture of Harpers Ferry; at Sharpsburg (Antietam) September 1862, he again assumed division command when General John R. Jones was incapacitated; General Starke was killed shortly thereafter. Brother of Confederate General Peter B. Starke.

Few Civil War combats proved more intense than this head-on confrontation between Fighting Joe Hooker and Stonewall Jackson. For about an hour and a half a gruesome struggle raged from the north end of the West Woods, through David Miller's thirty acre cornfield—famous ever afterward simply as "the Cornfield," the pasture south of it, and into the East Woods. The First Corps lost more than a quarter of its troops engaged in the battle. "Whole ranks went down," the commander of the Iron Brigade recounted, "and after we got possession of the field, dead men were piled on top of each other." Mounted on a white horse, Hooker himself made a fine target. About the time the First Corps became exhausted, its commander was wounded in the foot. Hooker's boot greatly slowed the bullet and in the excitement of battle, the general did not

## CLARISSA HARLOWE BARTON

Born Massachusetts 1821; at fifteen began teaching in district schools; later she organized a school for millworkers' children; in 1851 she studied at the Liberal Institute in New York; taught in Bordentown, N.J., where she persuaded the school board to institute free schooling; when opposition to a woman being in charge of such a large school arose and a male principal replaced her, Barton resigned and ended her teaching career; she moved to Washington, D.C., and obtained employment in the Patent Office. In 1861 she began her wartime service by helping supply the needs of the 6th Massachusetts Infantry Regiment, which had lost much of its baggage after being attacked by civilians while passing through Baltimore; thereafter she advertised for supplies to aid soldiers and received bountiful amounts which she distributed; in 1862 she secured permission to take provisions

realize he had been hit until he slumped from his horse. Taken back to the Pry house, the corps commander recovered from this wound and led the army the next spring during the Chancellorsville campaign.

Jackson's Corps suffered even more heavily than Hooker's. The total casualties in the divisions of Lawton and J.R. Jones came to roughly 40 percent of their numbers. General Lawton was wounded, one of his brigade commanders was killed, and two others were wounded. Jones's Division scored an equally grisly record: five of its brigade commanders suffered wounds. The division commander was wounded and his successor, Brigadier General William E. Starke, was hit by three bullets and died within an hour. Hood's Division paid a hideous price for its counterattack into the Cornfield. More than half of the

to the battlefields and to tend the wounded; thereafter she continued rendering heroic service by getting supplies to the front, distributing them, and ministering to the wounded; in 1864 she acted as superintendent of nurses with the Army of the James, but Barton never had any official connection with the army; although not primarily a hospital nurse, she secured supplies for the relief of suffering, and displayed courage, endurance, and resourcefulness on the battlefield. After the war she searched for missing soldiers and lectured on her wartime experiences; in 1869 she went abroad to recuperate from illness and became involved with the International Red Cross of Geneva, doing relief work under its auspices during the Franco-Prussian War for which she received honors from European royalty; after hard work she finally established the Red Cross in the U.S. in 1881; she spent the latter part of her life directing the organization until she resigned in 1904; she died at Glen Echo near Washington, D.C., in 1912. A slender woman, noted for her grit and determination, who squared her shoulders to any task, Barton spoke with authority and kept abreast of public affairs; her gift was the ability to see what needed to be done and to do it; her independent execution of operations sometimes caused controversy, but hard work and dedication earned her the title "angel of the battlefield."

soldiers of the 4th Texas Regiment, and over three-quarters of the 1st Texas, were killed or wounded. A survivor in Hampton's Legion told his parents after the battle: "Never have I seen men fall as fast and thick...I never saw rain fall faster than the bullets did around us."

From the onset of the battle, the wounded soldiers who were able to move streamed to the rear. During the days ahead every farmhouse, barn, and outbuilding in the area would be filled with suffering young men. At the beginning of the Maryland campaign Clarissa Harlowe Barton, a clerk in the Washington Patent Office until 1861, had collected a wagonload of medical supplies donated by citizens of the capital. When McClellan left Rockville in pursuit of Lee, this intrepid woman followed the Federal columns, certain that eventually the armies would come to battle and her aid would be needed. The morning's combat was raging when she arrived at a field hospital behind the Union lines and a surgeon greeted her with the exclamation: "God has indeed remembered us." Clara Barton's efforts would make the Antietam battlefield the birthplace of the American Red Cross.

The slaughter that opened the battle created enormous work for the surgeons, but little gain for the Federals. At 7:30 A.M. the Confederate lines were drawn back from where they had been at dawn, but only slightly. If Hooker's opening attack had been accompanied simultaneously with a similar advance by the Union left or center, McClellan might have been on his way to a decisive victory, early in the day. It was not to be. Watching the distant fighting from the Pry yard, the Young Napoleon was content to remark: "All goes well. Hooker is driving them."

# 7

# MANSFIELD FOLLOWS HOOKER

General Mansfield brought his Twelfth Corps up behind Hooker's and put it into the battle at about 7:30 A.M. By then the First Corps was exhausted and of little help to the fresh Union forces. Mansfield could see nothing better to do than deploy his corps much as Hooker had his. On the right, Brigadier General Alpheus S. Williams's division moved south toward the Cornfield and on the left, most of Brigadier General George S. Greene's division followed the line of the Smoketown Road toward the East Woods.

Mansfield, who had put in a long tenure with the Old Army before most of his young soldiers had been born, went into the battle with the van of his corps. Doubtless the War Department would have found him a suitable desk job in Washington, but the white-haired veteran wanted to serve under fire. Mansfield rode up to the 10th Maine in the East Woods, convinced the

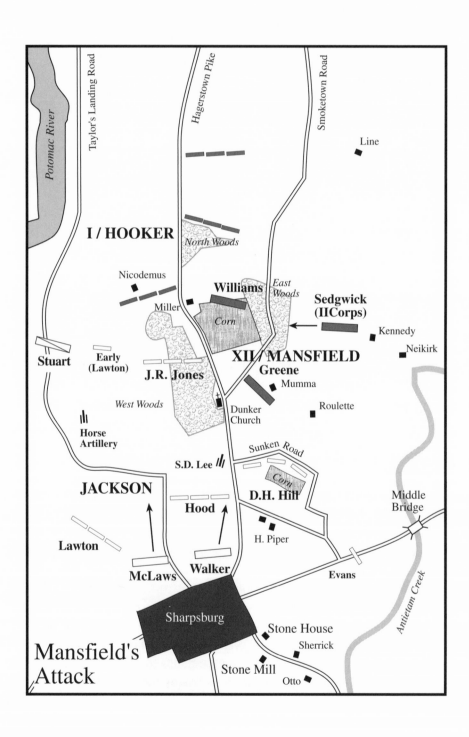

Mansfield's Attack

## GEORGE S. GREENE

Born Rhode Island 1801; graduated U.S. Military Academy second in his class of thirty-five in 1823; brevetted 2d lieutenant and posted to the 3rd Artillery; saw numerous garrison assignments; taught mathematics and engineering at West Point; 1st lieutenant 1829; resigned his commission in 1836 to pursue a career in civil engineering; engaged mostly in railroad construction; at the outbreak of the Civil War he was engineer in charge of the Croton Reservoir project in New York's Central Park; in January 1862, at sixty years of age, he offered his services to the Union and was commissioned colonel 66th New York Volunteer Infantry; promoted to brigadier general U.S. Volunteers April 1862; led brigade under General N.P. Banks in the Shenandoah Valley, seeing action at Cedar Mountain; ably commanded a division at Antietam; returning to  brigade command, he fought with distinction at Chancellorsville; at Gettysburg Greene's Brigade defended Culp's Hill against attacks that threatened Federal communications; transferred West with the Eleventh and Twelfth Corps; during the early stages of the Chattanooga Campaign October 1863, he was shot through the face at Wauhatchie and disabled until 1865; returned to lead a brigade in the Carolina Campaign; brevetted major general US Volunteers for war service, he was mustered out of the volunteers in 1866; returned to civil engineering, working in water supply, elevated trains, and street construction in New York City; worked on sewage and water supply projects in Washington, D.C., Detroit, and other cities; a founder and president of the American Society of Civil Engineers; keenly interested in genealogy and the affairs of the U.S. Military Academy, being for a long period that institution's oldest living graduate; father of *Monitor* executive officer Samuel Dana Greene; died at Morristown, New Jersey, 1899. General Greene was among the oldest field commanders in the war. A strict disciplinarian and a powerful motivator, he proved a competent and successful combat officer.

regiment was firing into other Union soldiers. "There are no Rebs," he yelled, "so far advanced." The New Englanders disagreed with their commander and some of them pointed toward the enemy. Mansfield leaned forward in his saddle, squinted, and finally conceded: "Yes, yes, you are right." The general had barely uttered this clause when a Confederate volley struck him and his mount. Some of Mansfield's men made a litter of their rifled muskets and carried him to the rear. Others later moved him by ambulance to the George Line house, where the Twelfth Corps had camped on the eve of the battle. Mansfield suffered through the night and died the next day.

General Williams succeeded the unfortunate Mansfield, Brigadier General Samuel W. Crawford in turn took over Williams's division, and the battle raged on. General Crawford pushed his men into the Cornfield, where they saw scenes of

## SAMUEL W. CRAWFORD

**Samuel W. Crawford:** born Pennsylvania 1829; after graduating from medical school University of Pennsylvania in 1851 took post in Southwest as assistant surgeon; in 1861 led a battery at Fort Sumter and made major 13th U.S. Infantry; in 1862 appointed brigadier general U.S. Volunteers; led a brigade at Winchester and Cedar Mountain; wounded at Antietam; in 1863 led a division at Gettysburg; in 1864 commanded a division and briefly the Fifth Corps during the Virginia campaigns; brevetted through major general in both U.S. and volunteer services; commissioned lieutenant colonel in 2d Infantry; after war served at various places in the South; promoted to colonel in 1869; retired in 1873 with the rank of brigadier general; died in Philadelphia in 1892.

horror left in the wake of the earlier fighting, and then encountered the soldiers that D.H. Hill had sent north from the Sunken Road to aid Stonewall Jackson. On Crawford's left, General Greene, a descendant of the famous Revolutionary War leader, directed most of his division into the East Woods. Pressed by Crawford and Greene, D.H. Hill's three brigades retreated south. Greene's men cleared the East Woods, moved down the Smoketown Road, and chased off S.D. Lee's field pieces. These Yankees had made a long advance and now they wisely lay down, taking cover behind the limestone rock outcroppings east of the Hagerstown Pike, across from the Dunker Church. One rookie regiment from Crawford's division, the 125th Pennsylvania, also made its way to this part of the field. This oversized unit crossed the Hagerstown Pike and, later supported by two New York regiments, ensconced itself in the West Woods.

By about 9 A.M. the attack of the Twelfth Corps had reached the end of its tether. The command's total losses eventually would come to nearly 1,900 officers and men, something over a quarter of its numbers engaged. In addition to General Mansfield, the corps lost one of Greene's brigade commanders, who was killed on the field. General Crawford and another of Greene's immediate subordinates were wounded. The Confederates also contributed further to the gruesome casualty rolls begun by Lawton, J.R. Jones, and Hood. The total losses in the three brigades of D.H. Hill's Division that advanced north from the Sunken Road probably approached 1,500 and included Brigadier General Roswell Ripley, who had been wounded in the neck.

As the morning's slaughter continued across the northern end of the battlefield, a tragic pattern emerged in the Union conduct of the engagement: the Federals were making bloody, but piecemeal, assaults. They were fighting the battle with one division, or at most two neighboring ones, under fire at a time. The Northern attacks were forceful enough to inflict horrible losses on their enemy, and on themselves, but never powerful enough to carry the field. Nor did McClellan ever stress Lee's already thin line by directing heavy forces against widely separated points along the Confederate front. By midmorning it was evident that the Union attacks were following a desolating course, which would produce a hideous slaughter but no conclusive results. Only one man, the commander of the Army of the Potomac, could change the pattern of the battle, but General McClellan instead allowed his corps commanders to fight a series of disjointed, fruitless combats.

# 8

## SEDGWICK'S CALAMITY

One of those officers, General Edwin V. Sumner, began pacing the lawn of the Pry yard at 6 A.M., waiting impatiently to see the army commander and get permission to lead the Second Corps into the battle. McClellan's staff kept the old soldier from seeing their chief, but after nearly an hour and a half the Young Napoleon granted the grizzled veteran the authority he wanted. Sumner rode back to his corps and ordered one of his divisions, commanded by the reliable Major General John Sedgwick, to ford the Antietam and move due west toward the East Woods. The old dragoon impetuously attached himself to this unit. Sumner's other two divisions, led by Brigadier General William H. French and Major General Israel B. Richardson, were to follow Sedgwick, but the corps commander left them on their own hook. Marching in columns, Sedgwick's men passed north of the Neikirk and Kennedy farms

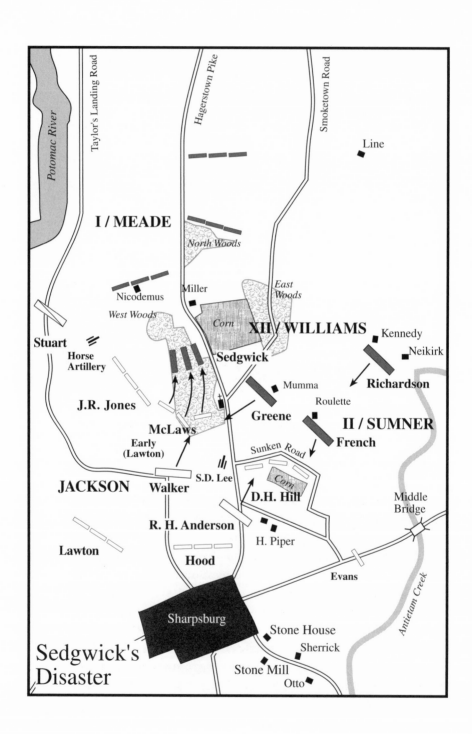

Sedgwick's Disaster

## JOHN SEDGWICK

Born Connecticut 1813; received his early education in the Connecticut common schools and a few months at an academy; he taught school before entering the U.S. Military Academy, from which he graduated twenty-fourth in his class in 1837; appointed 2d lieutenant in the 2d Artillery in 1837; promoted to 1st lieutenant in 1839; participated in the Seminole War, assisted in moving the Cherokee Indians west of the Mississippi, served on the northern frontier during the Canadian border disturbances, and on various garrison assignments; participated in the Mexican War; brevetted captain for gallant conduct in the battles of Contreras and Churubusco and major for gallant conduct in the action at Chapultepec; promoted to captain in 1849; after several years of garrison duty, he welcomed his appointment as major in the newly organized 1st Cavalry in 1855; participated in the Utah Expedition of 1857–58, and in the warfare with the Kiowa and Comanche

Indians, 1858–60; in 1861 he enjoyed quick promotions to lieutenant colonel of the 2d Cavalry, colonel of the 1st Cavalry, colonel of the 4th Cavalry, and finally brigadier general of volunteers; important assignments followed as brigade and then division commander in the Army of the Potomac; in 1862 he participated in most of the Peninsular Campaign, including Glendale where he was severely wounded; promoted to major general of volunteers in July 1862, he played a prominent role in the Battle of Antietam, where he was again wounded; he commanded for a time the Second Corps and the Ninth Corps, but in 1863 he led the Sixth Corps in the Chancellorsville, Fredericksburg, Salem Heights, Gettysburg, Rappahannock Station, and the Mine Run operations; in 1864, still commanding the Sixth Corps, he fought in the Wilderness and was killed by a Confederate sniper while directing the placing of artillery at Spotsylvania. Much loved by his men, this strict disciplinarian, a generous and affable bachelor, known to his troops as "Uncle John," was an able corps commander. He is buried in his native town, Cornwall Hollow, Connecticut.

## WILLIAM H. FRENCH

Born Maryland 1815; appointed to U.S. Military Academy from the District of Columbia; graduated 1837, twenty-second in his class of fifty cadets that included John Sedgwick, Joseph Hooker, Braxton Bragg, Jubal Early, and John Pemberton; brevetted 2d lieutenant and posted to artillery; served in Seminole wars; 1st lieutenant 1838; won two brevets for gallantry in Mexican War; captain 1848; at the outbreak of the Civil War he command- ed the Federal garrison at Eagle Pass, Texas, where he refused to follow General David E. Twiggs in surrendering Federal property to secessionist authorities; led his command to the mouth of the Rio Grande and there embarked for Key West; promoted to major U.S. Army and brigadier general U.S. Volunteers 1861; commanded a brigade in the Second Corps in the Peninsular Campaign and the Third Division of that corps at Antietam; major general U.S. Volunteers November 1862; led his division at Fredericksburg and Chancellorsville; during the Gettysburg Campaign he commanded the District of Harpers Ferry; ascended to command of the Third Corps following the wounding of General Daniel Sickles at Gettysburg; in the fall of 1863 he was criticized by General George G. Meade for his corps' slowness in exploiting a perceived opportunity to trap the enemy during the Mine Run operations; left without a command when the Third Corps was disbanded that winter in the Army of the Potomac reorganization; mustered out of the Volunteer organization in March 1864, he saw no further field service; brevetted through brigadier general U.S. Army for Fair Oaks, Antietam, and Chancellorsville and major general U.S. Army for war service; promoted to the full rank of lieutenant colonel in the regular army 1864; colonel 4th Artillery 1877; having retired from active duty 1880, General French died the following year. Known as a gifted artillerist, he had demonstrated solid command ability before the Mine Run accusations ruined his reputation.

and by 8:40 approached the East Woods. Sumner encountered an ambulance carrying Hooker back to the Pry house, but the semiconscious Fighting Joe could not tell the older general anything of the state of affairs at the front. Abandoning his responsibility as a corps commander, the eager dragoon relegated himself to the role of a division commander and pressed on toward the Confederate lines with Sedgwick's force alone.

Just beyond the East Woods, the division deployed from

## ISRAEL B. RICHARDSON

Born Vermont 1815; graduated U.S. Military Academy 1841, thirty-sixth in his class of fifty-two; breveted 2d lieutenant assigned to 3rd Infantry; fought in Seminole wars; 1st lieutenant 1846; served under both Generals Zachary Taylor and Winfield Scott in Mexico, winning two brevets for gallantry and the sobriquet "Fighting Dick"; on frontier duty mostly in the Southwest; captain 1851; resigned commission 1855 to farm in Michigan; at the outbreak of the Civil War he organized the 2d Michigan Volunteer Infantry, becoming its colonel; skillfully covered the Federal retreat at First Bull Run August 1861, and was promoted brigadier general U.S. Volunteers shortly thereafter; commanded a division in the Peninsular Campaign spring 1862; major general U.S. Volunteers July 1862; led a division in General Edwin Vose Sumner's Second Corps at South Mountain and Antietam September 1862; at Antietam his division was instrumental in driving the Rebels from the "Bloody Lane" in some of the war's fiercest fighting; while directing this action  General Richardson was severely wounded; he died in November. Known as a strong organizer and disciplinarian, he was exceedingly popular with his men, inspiring them by his own example.

columns into lines. Sedgwick's men had reached the front at a time when the Southern defenders were exhausted by their fight against the First and the Twelfth Corps. A relative quiet prevailed, broken by an occasional shot from a rifle or cannon, or the unnerving sounds made by wounded men and horses. Lee's left flank had been shattered by the morning's battle and it was possible that a powerful Union attack now might gain the breakthrough that had eluded Hooker and Mansfield.

Sumner and Sedgwick led the long lines of dark blue-coated infantrymen west, through the Cornfield. Here they encountered carnage beyond description, the dead and the dying left in the path of the earlier combat. Some of Sedgwick's men, pitying the unfortunate wounded men they found among the trampled cornstalks, stepped from their ranks and offered their canteens to the agonized Northerners and Southerners alike. Colonel Norman James Hall of the 7th Michigan stopped to encourage one of his enemies, a veteran of Hood's Division. "You fought and stood well," the Union regimental commander told his foe. "Yes," the Rebel answered, "and here we lie."

Sedgwick's troops could do little for any of the maimed soldiers they found in the Cornfield and they marched on toward their own grim fate. Advancing in six long lines, each of the three brigades in two ranks, the division of roughly 5,400 attackers presented an imposing sight. The Federal veterans clambered over the post and rail fence which bordered the sides of the Hagerstown Pike, crossed the open field west of that road, and sometime after 9 A.M. entered the northern stretch of the West Woods. Sedgwick's front-line brigade almost immediately began a fire fight with some of Stonewall Jackson's men, survivors of the combat earlier that morning. Behind this lead brigade, the other two came to a halt.

In his anxiety to get his corps into the battle, Sumner had made at least three mistakes. First, he had advanced with scant intelligence of the location and condition of the Confederate, and Union, units he would find at the front.

Second, riding with his lead division, the former dragoon had lost all communication with the other two. Finally, Sedgwick's unit deployed from its marching columns into close-order lines with short intervals between its brigades. This was a standard formation of its day and was as suitable as any, if the division met resistance only in its front. If, however, the Confederates struck Sedgwick's close-order lines in the flank, the Federals would have little chance of defending themselves. And this was precisely what happened.

Sedgwick's division had advanced westward across the northern part of the battlefield after the First and the Twelfth Corps had battered the Confederate left. At the time this Union formation had crossed the Cornfield, there were few organized Southern units of any size along that part of the front. Some of Stuart's cavalrymen still were deployed to the north and a few remnants of Jackson's Corps tried to resist Sedgwick's lead brigade. The Confederate forces in front of this fresh, veteran Second Corps division had been drained by the earlier fighting and under other circumstances the Federals might have smashed through Lee's weakened line and carried the day. But while Sedgwick's front brigade engaged Jackson's survivors and while the two brigades behind it stood at a halt, Southern reinforcements were closing on their left flank. Lee's aide, Major Walter H. Taylor, had given Lafayette McLaws an order to bring his men up from the fields north of the village, where they had been resting that morning. Not far behind, John Walker advanced with another Southern division, which, unneeded on the Confederate right, shifted to bolster Lee's hard-hit left.

While Sedgwick's front-line brigade fired at Jackson's remnants and while the two brigades behind it awaited orders, McLaws's Division pressed north on a collision course with their vulnerable left flank. The trees of the West Woods prevented the Federals from seeing this Confederate advance. One minute, the soldiers in Sedgwick's middle and rear brigades stood idly, their officers lighting up pipes and cigars; the next, disaster struck them. The Southerners suddenly opened up against three sides of Sedgwick's division, the heaviest fire coming from the left, where McLaws's men seized their opportunity.

Caught in its close ordered formation, one of the finest divisions in the Federal army dissolved in a matter of minutes. "Our three lines, each in two ranks, were so near together," one of the unit's hapless brigade commanders later recalled, "that a rifle bullet would often cross them all and disable five or six men at a time." The total losses—killed, wounded, and missing—in Sedgwick's division during the Battle of Antietam came to 2,210 and most of these casualties were suffered in this disaster in the West Woods. The slaughter took place, as one officer put it, in "less time than it takes to tell it." A bullet hit General Sedgwick in the leg, knocking him out of his saddle, and later, while still trying to rally his men, he suffered two more wounds. Many of the survivors among his ranks retreated across the Nicodemus and Miller farms to the shelter of the North Woods, taking with them the 125th Pennsylvania and other remnants of the morning's battle.

In the wake of Sedgwick's disaster, the Federals made another of their spasmodic advances. Greene's men moved from the rock outcroppings east of the Dunker Church and pressed into the West Woods, but they were the only sizeable Union force left on this part of the battlefield. Their commander later described their isolated position, in words that well represented the experience of other Federal divisions on that day. "We were in advance of our line," Greene reported, "on the right and left of us.... I placed the division in line, with the right thrown back, and sent forward skirmishers and sought reinforcements from General Williams. None were at the time available."

While the disconnected actions of Sedgwick's and Greene's divisions typified the futility of McClellan's piecemeal attacks, the timely arrival of McLaws's and Walker's units illustrated one motif of Lee's successful defense. Although the Army of Northern Virginia was desperately outnumbered, its interior lines helped its commander shift units quickly from quiet parts of the battlefield to meet the series of disjointed Federal attacks one at a time. And while McClellan remained at the Pry house, leaving his corps and division commanders to fight their disorganized combats, Lee spent the day moving from one point to another along his threadbare front, personally directing his officers and men.

# 9

# THE SUNKEN ROAD

General French's division now came to the front and continued the tragically futile pattern of the Northern attacks. This unit should have supported Sedgwick's brigades and might have ameliorated their fate, but Sumner failed to keep track of its route across the battlefield. Historians have never determined for certain why French did not follow Sedgwick west toward the West Woods and why, instead, he led his men southwest against the Sunken Road.

Nature, not Confederate engineering, had made this country lane one of the strongest defensive positions of the war. Heavy use by farm wagons and persistent erosion by Maryland rains over the years had created a natural field entrenchment. This long road was held by part of D.H. Hill's Division, reinforced by R.H. Anderson's. Harvey Hill's soldiers further strengthened their naturally fortified line by piling fence rails to improvise a line of breastworks, but the position did have at

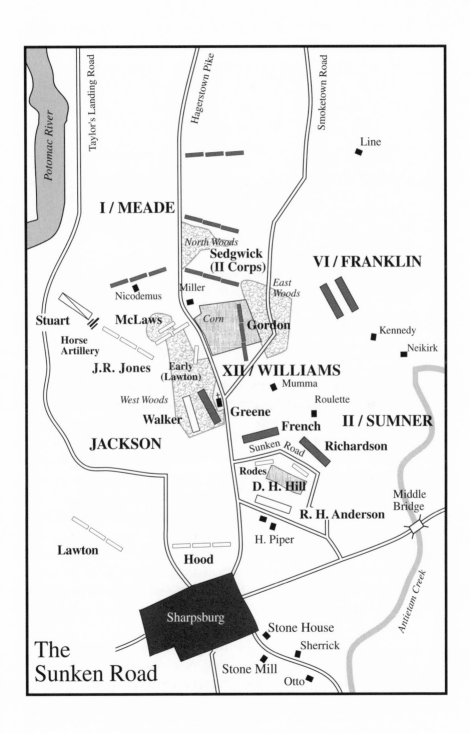

The
Sunken Road

least one weakness: the Union attackers would hold higher ground than the defenders down in the Sunken Road.

Sometime after 9 A.M., General French brought his division south past the Roulette farm toward this zigzagging lane, the center of the Army of Northern Virginia. Hill's men let them close within deadly range and then opened a volley that devastated the front line of the Union advance. The Federals prudently took cover by lying down along the crest and maintained a fire against the Confederates in the road. The Southerners fought equally stubbornly from the protection of their ditch-and-rails defenses. Neither side would give way. The 8th Ohio fought persistently in front of the Sunken Road and the Confederates riddled its regimental flag with bullets. The next day Lieutenant Colonel Franklin Sawyer recounted the unit's courageous performance: "During the entire engagement my officers and men behaved with the utmost bravery and gallantry; not a man gave way. Our colors received seventeen balls, but were never once depressed during the storm of battle." Many commanders on both sides truthfully could have claimed that their own units fought with the same determination during this stubborn combat along the Sunken Road.

About 10 A.M. the last fresh division of the Second Corps, Israel Richardson's, closed on French's left. Brigadier General Thomas Francis Meagher's Irish Brigade led the renewed Federal assault, advancing with Celtic aggressiveness. Its leader later reported that he intended to deliver a bayonet charge, "relying on the impetuosity and recklessness of Irish soldiers in a charge." Scores of Meagher's troops were shot down within a matter of minutes and eventually their total losses came to about 540 officers and men. The 69th New York lost more than 60 percent of its numbers, and the 63rd New York nearly the same.

General Richardson, one of the most combative leaders in the Union army, pressed the rest of his division into the fight for the Sunken Road. He advanced on foot, sword in hand, posting his artillery, cursing his officers, and urging his men to advance. Told that one of his brigadiers had remained in the rear, Richardson exploded: "God damn the field officers!"

The Confederate defense of the Sunken Road began to unravel when the Federals put the 6th Alabama, posted near a

## THOMAS FRANCIS MEAGHER

Born Ireland 1823; leader in Irish independence movements; banished to Tasmania for sedition by the British government 1849; escaped to United States 1852; eventually locating in New York, where he became an influential member of that city's Irish-American community; a lecturer, newspaper editor, and lawyer; at the outbreak of the Civil War he organized a zouave company as part of the 69th New York Volunteer Infantry, becoming the regiment's major; fought at First Bull Run but returned to New York where he organized and was elected to command the Irish Brigade; commissioned brigadier general U.S. Volunteers February 1862; saw heavy fighting during the Peninsular Campaign, Second Bull Run, Antietam, and Fredericksburg 1862; resigned May 1863 following Chancellosville when the army threatened to break up the shattered Irish Brigade; his resignation rejected, he was sent West in 1864; commanded District of the Etowah and later joined General W.T. Sherman's command in Georgia, engaged mostly in rear area duties; stationed at Savannah, he resigned May 1865; appointed territorial secretary of Montana and served there as temporary governor; in a bizarre event at Fort Benton, Montana, he fell from a river steamer and apparently drowned in the Missouri River 1867; his body was never  recovered. Although he saw some of the war's fiercest fighting on behalf of the Union, General Meagher's chief concern remained advancing the cause of Irish independence.

## ROBERT EMMETT RODES

Born Virginia 1829, the son of a militia general; graduated from the Virginia Military Institute, tenth in the class of 1848; received faculty appointment at his alma mater, 1848–49; after working as a civil engineer throughout the South and Southwest, became chief engineer on an Alabama railroad, and married Virginia H. Woodruff of Tuscaloosa; he and his wife were traveling

in Europe when the Civil War began; Rodes returned to Alabama and received command of the 5th Alabama Infantry, which he led to defend Virginia. He saw no fighting at First Manassas, but received promotion to brigadier after the battle; in 1862 his brigade suffered heavy casualties at Seven Pines, where he received a severe wound and a superior officer described him as "a capital officer." Rodes returned to duty in time to fight courageously during the Antietam Campaign where he was again wounded; he took little part in the action at Fredericksburg, but in 1863 played a major role in the flank attack at Chancellorsville, succeeding first to Hill's Division and then to Jackson's Corps, which Rodes turned over to Jeb Stuart. Promoted to major general and given command of a division, he received some criticism for his activities at Gettysburg, but served nobly in 1864 during actions in the Wilderness and Spotsylvania; accompanied Jubal Early in June 1864 to the Shenandoah Valley; fought at Kernstown, on the Washington raid, at Monocacy, and at Winchester, where on September 19, 1864, a bullet in the head killed him. Contemporaries considered Rodes "brilliant" and reported him "much admired... and very popular"; indeed, one of the "most splendid looking soldiers of the war." "Rodes was the best Division commander in the Army of N. Va.," said General Early, "& was worthy of & capable for any position in it."

bend in the lane, under a heavy fire. To answer this threat, Brigadier General Robert Rodes ordered the regiment to throw back its right flank, but Lieutenant Colonel J. N. Lightfoot mistook this as an order for his entire unit to pull out of the road.

## FRANCIS CHANNING BARLOW

Born New York 1834; graduated first in his class at Harvard in 1855; studied and then practised law along with editorial work for the *New York Tribune*; in 1861 he enlisted as private in the 12th New York Militia and the following day married Arabella Wharton Griffith; a month latter he was appointed 1st lieutenant, but honorably mustered out three months later; became lieutenant colonel of the 61st New York Militia; promotion to colonel in 1862, Barlow participated in the siege of Yorktown and distinguished himself at Fair Oaks; commanding a brigade in the battle of Antietam, Barlow was wounded; promoted to brigadier general; at Chancellorsville in 1863 his brigade was routed; wounded and left paralyzed on the battlefield at Gettysburg, where Confederate General John B. Gordon found him, gave him water, and brought him to safety; on rejoining the Federal army, Barlow commanded a division in the Second Corps in 1864 during action in the Wilderness, Spotsylvania (for which he was brevetted major general), Cold Harbor, and Petersburg; he took leave of absence because of ill health returning to command a division at Sayler's Creek and Farmville in 1865; after this duty Barton was promoted major general and served with his command until his resignation in late 1865; he  resumed his law practice and helped found the American Bar Association; as a Republican he participated in politics and was New York attorney general in the prosecution of "Boss" Tweed and his henchmen; he died in New York 1896. Boyish in build and stature, Barton nevertheless commanded respect in his public and military career, fulfilling his duties with energy and enthusiasm.

Major E. L. Hobson, who commanded the regiment to the left of the 6th Alabama, asked Colonel Lightfoot if the command was intended for all of the brigade. Lightfoot gave him an affirmative answer and Hobson ordered his own regiment to retreat. A chain reaction ran along the lane and soon Rodes' entire brigade began abandoning its line. The Federals, from their higher ground, shot many of the Alabamians in the back as they scrambled up the bank, out of the Sunken Road and into the cornfield of the Henry Piper farm.

As Rodes's Brigade mistakenly retreated, Colonel Francis C. Barlow, commanding the 61st and 64th New York, took advantage of the Southern error. The Harvard lawyer pressed his

## JOHN BROWN GORDON

Born Georgia 1832; attended University of Georgia, but did not graduate; studied law; in 1856 entered his father's coal mining business; quickly became wealthy and entered politics; a southern rights Democrat, who favored secession; in 1861 he raised a company that joined the 6th Alabama Infantry, which elected him major; served but saw no action at First Manassas; promoted to colonel of the 6th Alabama and in 1862 transferred to General Robert E. Rodes's Brigade; during the Peninsular Campaign, after Rodes was wounded, Gordon commanded the brigade at Gaines' Mill and Malvern Hill; participated in the battles at South Mountain and Sharpsburg, where five bullets struck him; his wife, who had left their two sons with her mother-in-law in Georgia, nursed him back to health; promoted to brigadier general, he commanded a brigade in Jubal A. Early's Division. "Not to promote him," said E.P. Alexander, "would have been a scandal." In 1863 Gordon won the respect of his men at Chancellorsville and Gettysburg; in 1864 at the Wilderness he delivered a

regiments up to the lane, where they gained a flanking fire against the 4th North Carolina. More than 300 of the Sunken Road's defenders surrendered to the New Yorkers and the 61st captured three Confederate battle flags. The National troops crossed the lane, which now was thick with the dead and maimed. According to local tradition, an elderly woman who lived nearby visited this hideous scene shortly after the battle and gave the Sunken Road the name it has carried ever since, the Bloody Lane.

The Federals had ripped open the center of the Southern line, jeopardizing Lee's army and the entire Confederate nation. It may well be that the Army of Northern Virginia stood

crushing attack on the Union right; at Spotsylvania, commanding a division, his counterattack saved Lee's army; promoted to major general in May, he served under Early in the Shenandoah Valley Campaign, forcing General David O. Hunter from the valley and defeating General Lew Wallace at Monocacy; after failing to take Washington, D.C., Gordon and Early's Corps lost battles in September at Winchester and Fisher's Hill; a month later at Cedar Creek, Gordon executed a magnificent flanking movement, but his inability to control his hungry troops, who pillaged abandoned Yankee camps, outraged Early; their relationship deteriorated and hostility continued into the postwar years; in December Gordon rejoined Lee's forces defending Petersburg; in 1865 he directed an attack on Fort Stedman and then commanded the Second Corps on the retreat to Appomattox; after the war he served in the US Senate from 1873 to 1880 and from 1881 to 1897 and as governor of Georgia from 1886 to 1890; engaged in various business interests; served as commander-in-chief of the United Confederate Veterans; published *Reminiscences of the Civil War* in 1903; he died in 1904. Six feet tall, thin, but with perfect posture, Gordon inspired confidence; officers called him "a picture for the sculptor" and "the very personification of a hero." But an admiring soldier offered the best description: "He's most the prettiest thing you ever did see on a field of fight. It'ud put fight into a whipped chicken just to look at him!"

in greater peril after the Union breakthrough across the Bloody Lane than it ever did again until the final weeks of the Civil War. D.H. Hill's men had paid an enormous price for their defense against French and Richardson. After one brigade commander, Brigadier General George B. Anderson, was mortally wounded, Colonel Charles C. Tew succeeded him and was shot dead by a bullet in the head. Tew fell while talking with Colonel John Brown Gordon of the 6th Alabama, who himself eventually suffered five wounds. The losses in the brigades of George B. Anderson and Robert Rodes included more than 500 killed and wounded, and the division of R.H. Anderson over 1,000 wounded, including the commander himself and two other general officers. The Confederate line stretched so thinly across the Piper farm that a division commander, Major General D.H. Hill, handled a musket and a corps commander, Lieutenant General Longstreet, held the horses of his staff officers while they manned some cannon whose gun crews had been shot down. Lee had no reserves left on the field and earnestly awaited the arrival of A.P. Hill's Division, now en route from Harpers Ferry.

At first it seemed the Federals would not be able to exploit the advantage they had gained at the center of the battlefield. To the right of French, Walker's division drove the remnants of Greene's men from their outpost in the West Woods shortly after noon. Furthermore, the Union troops which had won the battle for the Bloody Lane had paid a frightful cost for their success. French's division suffered more heavily that day than any comparable Union unit except one, Sedgwick's, with its traumatic casualties in the West Woods. Richardson's losses also had been severe and the commander himself was mortally wounded. Struck in the shoulder by a shell fragment, this hard driving division leader was carried to an upstairs bedroom of the Pry house, where he died six weeks later.

The Federal army had taken appalling casualties but, unlike its opponent, still had reserves. The cavalry division, the Sixth Corps, and two divisions of the Fifth Corps were fresh and at hand. Shortly after noon General Pleasonton brought his horse artillery and most of his troopers across the Middle Bridge to the west bank of the Antietam, where they remained until the end of the battle. The two divisions of General Franklin's Sixth Corps arrived on the field during the middle of the day and relieved the exhausted survivors of the Twelfth and Second Corps. Some battalions of Brigadier General George Sykes's division of the Fifth Corps crossed the Antietam to support Pleasonton's horse batteries and, late in the afternoon, these Regulars skirmished their way along the Boonsboro Pike toward Sharpsburg.

The Army of the Potomac had fresh troops, but the question remained whether its commander would use them. At about 2 P.M. McClellan rode to the front with a few of his staff officers. When the army commander arrived there, he listened, unfortunately for the National cause, to the counsel of General Sumner, probably the most demoralized Federal senior officer on the field. The "Bull of the Woods" was usually an agressive commander, but his experience during Sedgwick's disaster had crushed his fighting spirit. Sumner convinced the cautious McClellan, who was easily persuaded, to make no further attacks on that part of the field. Little Mac returned to the Pry house and Lee's threadbare line was spared what might well have been a fatal blow.

McClellan's caution contrasted sharply with his opponent's aggressive defense. While the Union leader benefited from enormous advantages but hesitated to exploit them, Lee had withstood fearful attacks and yet wanted to seize the initiative. This Southern leader demonstrated his fighting spirit during his most famous tactical offensives, at Second Manassas, Chancellorsville, and Gettysburg—and he also did so during this defensive battle at Sharpsburg. After his line had been battered all morning, his reserves exhausted, and his center driven in, the heavily outnumbered Confederate commander did what few generals would have considered: he looked for a way to attack. If the terrain and Union dispositions had allowed it, Lee and Jackson might well have carried out at Sharpsburg the same kind of tactical envelopment they executed the following spring at Chancellorsville. Lee later reported that while the Federals attacked his center, he had ordered Jackson to turn the Union right flank. The aggressive Stonewall told one of the Confederate division commanders that afternoon, "We'll drive McClellan into the Potomac." Lee explained afterward that the Southern leaders learned that the Union right extended "nearly to the Potomac, and [was] so strongly defended with artillery that the attempt had to be abandoned."

# 10

## BURNSIDE'S BRIDGE

The Confederates reluctantly gave up their intention to attack the northern end of McClellan's line and the main action of the battle shifted to the south, to the Lower Bridge across the Antietam. Here a few hundred Georgians led by Brigadier General Robert Toombs had stymied all morning Major General Burnside's entire Ninth Corps. The defenders were overwhelmingly outnumbered, but they held better ground than the Federals and their shoulder arms fire commanded the stone bridge and its approaches.

The Antietam ran relatively low that autumn and critics later claimed that the Federals could have forded it more easily than they realized. Fording, however, depended as much on the condition of the banks as on the depth of the water. Further, the Union task was not to pass a handful of men across the creek, but a corps of 13,800, with their paper car-

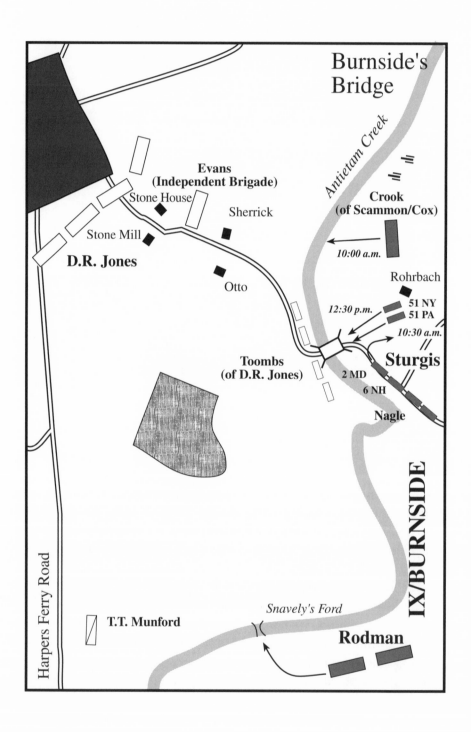

tridges dry and with the wagons that carried their additional ammunition. Whatever his reasons, Burnside focused his attention on the Lower Bridge rather than its neighboring fords.

The Battle of Antietam ended the close friendship between McClellan and Burnside. Each officer blamed the other for the dismal Union performance against the Lower Bridge, and both men had strong grounds for their complaints. McClellan failed to make clear to his subordinate exactly what he wanted him to do, and how his operations fit into the army commander's larger plan for the entire battle. Little Mac himself seemed uncertain whether Burnside's operation was to be a main

## ISAAC P. RODMAN

Born Rhode Island 1822; prominent businessman and state legislator; although a Quaker he became a captain in the 2d Rhode Island Volunteer Infantry following the outbreak of the Civil War; heavily engaged at First Bull Run; resigned to become colonel 4th Rhode Island Volunteer Infantry October 1861; in General Ambrose Burnside's Carolina expedition; fought conspicuously at Roanoke Island, New Bern, and Fort Macon; stricken with typhoid fever he returned to Rhode Island; appointed brigadier general U.S. Volunteers April 1862; rejoining his command in September, he assumed direction of a division in the Ninth Corps, Army of the Potomac, temporarily headed by General Jesse Reno; fought at South Mountain; at Antietam, September 17, during the day-long fight for "Burnside's Bridge," Rodman managed to get his division across Antietam Creek and was advancing on Sharpsburg just as General A.P. Hill's Confederate division arrived on the scene; in the ensuing melee General Rodman was mortally wounded; he died two weeks later.

attack, or secondary to the one by the forces on the Federal right. The night before the battle, McClellan visited Burnside's headquarters. He did not order his subordinate to advance at dawn, in concert with Hooker, but merely to position his troops that evening and attack in the morning, when ordered. Burnside, for his part, gave no energy to the operation and remained content to pass on McClellan's orders to Cox and to let events take their ponderous course. The ultimate responsibility for the delays and failures, however, rested with the army commander. If he wanted Burnside to make a vigorous advance, he should have insisted on it. The Pry house stood about two miles from the Lower Bridge. A more forceful leader than McClellan—Robert E. Lee or Stonewall Jackson—would have ridden to the scene and directed the attack himself.

The Union army commander did not dispatch an order to Burnside to open his attack until 9:10 A.M., more than three hours after Hooker had engaged Lee's left, and about three and a half hours after dawn. It was nearly 10 A.M., while Richardson was advancing to help French carry the Sunken Road, when one of McClellan's staff officers delivered this directive to Burnside, who grandly passed it on to General Cox. The order went down the chain of command and Brigadier General Isaac P. Rodman set off with his division to find a way to ford the Antietam farther downstream, while Colonel George Crook readied his brigade for a direct attack on the bridge.

This Ohio officer had fought against the Indians and would do so again after the war, gaining fame for his operations in the Southwest against the Apaches, but he won no glory for his performance at the Antietam. Inexperienced with brigade operations, Crook failed to send out any skirmishers to scout his front. His men lunged at the bridge, landed their attack too far north of it, and came under the rifles of the Confederates from their commanding position on the opposite side of the creek. Crook's Buckeyes lay down on the east bank, taking what cover they could and returning the fire of the defenders, but unable to do anything more.

At about 10:30 A.M., while General Rodman's division tramped downstream to look for a ford, the 2d Maryland and 6th New Hampshire mounted another effort against the Lower Bridge. Moving in a column of fours, the Federals trotted up the road that ran alongside the Antietam to the bridge. As soon as the attackers came out into the open, the Georgians on the high ground on the far bank opened a devastating fire into their left flank. The bluecoats scattered for cover, the lead regiment losing more than 40 percent of its numbers. When the noon hour approached, Robert Toombs could boast that his few hundred defenders had held a Union corps of four divisions at bay for half a day.

It was not until the early afternoon that fortune shifted to the Federals. Shortly after midday Rodman's division began crossing Snavely's Ford, which would put this unit on the west bank of the Antietam, behind Toombs's right flank. At about the same time Brigadier General Edward Ferrero readied the 51st Pennsylvania and the 51st New York for yet another assault against the Lower Bridge. These regiments profited from the experience of their predecessors. Like the Maryland and New Hampshire units, Ferrero's men used storm column tactics, but unlike them, they did not take the road which paralleled the stream. Instead, the Pennsylvanians and New Yorkers charged down from the slope opposite the bridge and directly at it, reducing the length of their approach and denying the defenders a flanking fire.

This attack carried the three-arch stone span, famous afterward as "Burnside's Bridge," while Rodman's division made its way north from Snavely's Ford, threatening the right and rear of the Georgian defenders. Toombs's men, outflanked and by now low on ammunition, retreated half a mile west. The Ninth Corps at last had uncorked the bottleneck at the bridge, but Burnside now used two invaluable hours reorganizing his forces, bringing units and ammunition across the Antietam.

Shortly after 3 P.M. the Nationals began their advance against the slender Confederate right flank and, despite all of the frustrations and delays, a decisive Union victory seemed imminent. Burnside had at hand about 8,500 soldiers, while Lee had left only one division which could oppose them, Brigadier General David R. Jones's modest command of about 2,800 infantrymen. These Southerners were extended along a meager front around the edge of Sharpsburg, covering the eastern and southeastern approaches to the village. "We were now left to oppose the numerous masses before us," wrote one Rebel private, "with a mere picket line of musketry." Just to the southwest, not far behind the thin Confederate line, were the shallows in the Potomac River at Boteler's Ford and Lee's vital route back into Virginia.

The Ninth Corps seized its opportunity. On the left General Rodman urged his men into battle, the right of his division advancing toward the Harpers Ferry Road and the left moving into a forty-acre cornfield at the far southern end of the Union line. On the right, Brigadier General Orlando B. Willcox's Division cleared the Sherrick and Otto farmhouses and the stone mill beyond them and fought its way to the southeastern edge of Sharpsburg. Union shells rained down on the streets and buildings of the village. By 4 P.M. the Army of Northern Virginia stood once more at the edge of disaster. Lee had only one remaining hope: Major General A.P. Hill's Division, which had left Harpers Ferry at about 7:30 A.M., roughly the time that Mansfield's Twelfth Corps had begun its attack.

# 11

## HILL RESCUES LEE

The red bearded and contentious A. P. Hill pushed his men north to join the rest of the Army of Northern Virginia, covering seventeen miles in less than eight hours. Although hundreds in the ranks could not maintain that pace and fell by the wayside between Harpers Ferry and Sharpsburg, Powell Hill brought a considerable force, something over 3,000 soldiers, to Lee's aid. Moreover, they arrived at the perfect time and place. Splashing across Boteler's Ford and pressing up Miller's Sawmill Road, the Light Division struck the left flank of the Ninth Corps and reversed the course of the battle, driving the Federals back toward Burnside's Bridge.

For the men who fought on the southern end of the battlefield, the experience was as intense as for those in the Cornfield, the West Woods, or along the Bloody Lane. The Ninth Corps, which had fallen just short of breaking Lee's right

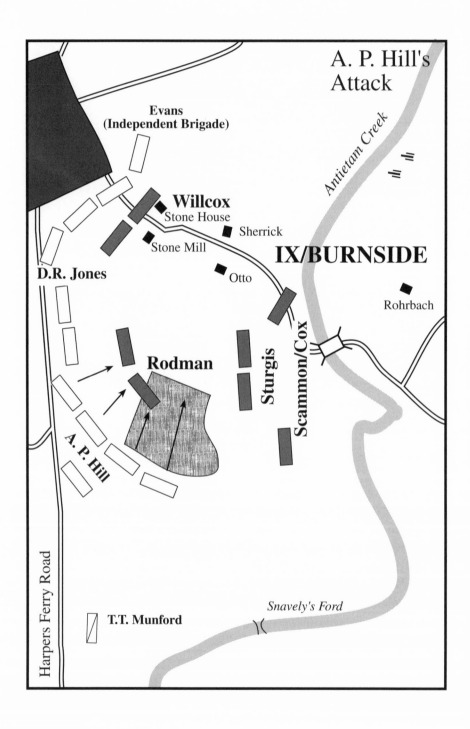

flank, suffered about 2,500 total casualties. General Rodman was mortally wounded in the chest, shot from his saddle when the Confederates took his division in the flank. David R. Jones's Division lost heavily, too, its total accounting coming to almost 1,200. The casualties in A.P. Hill's Division, which enjoyed the advantage of its tactical position, were merciful by the standards of that gruesome day, but they included one of the Light Division's brigadiers, Lawrence O'Brien Branch, killed by a bullet through the head.

The blood red sun finally dropped to the horizon, bringing an end to the day's ghastly work. The gun crews ceased fire and their cannon barrels began to cool in the September evening. Across the battlefield, the shoulder-arms fire faded to isolated shooting and finally died in the darkness. McClellan's disjointed attacks had created enormous suffering, but no decisive results. By the closest of margins, Lee had held his army together.

# 12

## AFTER THE SLAUGHTER

The Battle of Antietam was over, but the torments of the wounded continued for weeks. The exhausted Southern survivors looked for their stricken comrades long into the night and where they were able, dressed their wounds, and put the unfortunates into wagons. Both armies left thousands of maimed soldiers in the fields and farmlots. "From Hagerstown to the southern limits of [Washington] county," one local newspaper reported a week after the terrible battle, "wounded and dying are to be found in every neighborhood and in nearly every house. The whole region of country between Boonsboro and Sharpsburg is one vast hospital." Long after the war, a veteran of the 76th New York recounted his work as a hospital steward in a church on the edge of the battlefield. "During the day when I could get a few moments to spare," he recalled, "I was writing letters from the pulpit to those dear ones at home, for those who lay there with mangled limbs and bodies.... I presume that the congregation that now worships God in the brick church at Keedysville, little realize that once upon a time the church was filled with men packed in nearly as thick as sardines in a box, and each minus a limb, while some had five or six dangerous wounds, and that for a while every morning from one to five would be carried out a corpse."

The precise extent of the carnage would never be known. One historian who made a thorough study of the evidence put the total Northern losses at about 12,800 and the Southern at roughly 11,500, producing a combined figure of 24,300. No one could imagine the anguish these statistics represented. During the weeks after the battle, countless families would learn that their son would never return to his farmhouse in New York or his log cabin in Georgia. Other Civil War combats—Chickamauga, Gettysburg, the Seven Days' Battles—produced even larger casualties, but none in so short a period of time. Antietam was the bloodiest single day of this or any other American war.

The two armies had pounded each other to exhaustion. Lee had scarcely held his army together through the Battle of Sharpsburg and well might have retreated the night of the seventeenth. Yet he remained on the field the day after the battle, risking still again the possibility that the Federals, with their larger numbers, would deliver a fatal blow. Lee had to collect his wounded and allow his men, drained by marching and combat, to eat and rest. Further, the Southern commander believed that his small, battered army could remain in place safely. As he had throughout the campaign, Lee acted on the confident assumption that McClellan always would exercise caution.

Despite its frightful battle losses, the Army of the Potomac still greatly outnumbered its foe and, unlike its opponent, it had troops in reserve. General Darius N. Couch's Fourth Corps division now was at hand and General Andrew A. Humphreys

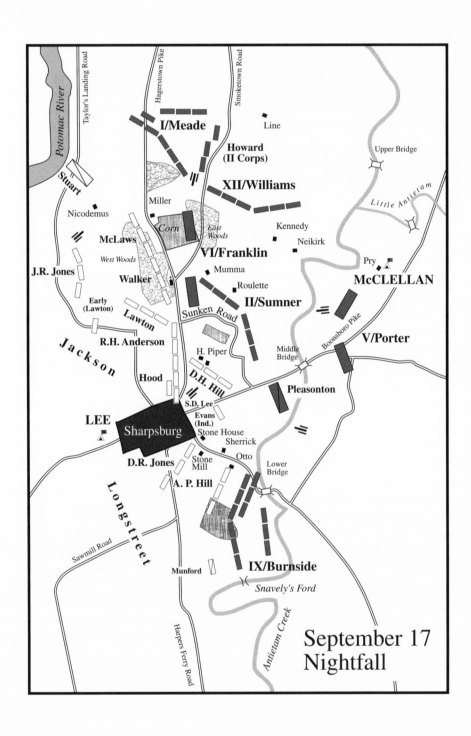

September 17
Nightfall

had brought his division to join the other two of the Fifth Corps, which had seen very little action on the seventeenth. Other than Colonel William H. Irwin's brigade, which had launched an isolated, futile foray late in the battle, the entire Sixth Corps remained fresh. These commands gave the Union army a striking force of more than two combat-ready corps, supported by ample artillery and cavalry. Yet McClellan, just as Lee expected, and just as he had on the sixteenth, took no initiative on September 18.

During the night of the eighteenth and nineteenth, the Southerners at last retreated across the Potomac. A single brigade of cavalry, commanded by the army commander's nephew, Brigadier General Fitzhugh Lee, covered the dejected soldiers and the wagonloads of wounded as they crossed Boteler's Ford. Within about two hours after sunrise on the nineteenth, the last of the Confederates were back in Virginia.

On September 19 Fitz John Porter put a detachment of his Fifth Corps across the river and captured a few field guns. The next morning A. P. Hill mounted a rearguard action that drove the pursuers back across the Potomac. The rookie 118th Pennsylvania, the Corn Exchange regiment, learned to its horror that about half its Enfield rifles were defective. Its colonel was severely wounded, and the hapless unit lost nearly 270 casualties during this final encounter of the Antietam campaign. The Confederates then continued their retreat, toward Martinsburg.

While Lee's soldiers moved back into Virginia, photographers were already at work on the Antietam battlefield. Alexander Gardner and James F. Gibson, dispatched from Washington by Mathew Brady, recorded a series of grim images of death and destruction, the residue of the violence near Sharpsburg. No American battlefield had ever been photographed so extensively, and so soon after the combat ended. Brady exhibited these Antietam photographs in New York City and many civilians were haunted by the merciless scenes, which contrasted sharply with the romantic engravings that appeared in their newspapers. This exhibition foreshadowed the mass media coverage of warfare in the twentieth century, when Americans would watch the Vietnam and Gulf wars on their televisions.

The Battle of Antietam had been a gruesome stalemate, but the campaign proved a decisive Union victory. After Lee's battered units had returned to Virginia, one of his brigade commanders wrote: "I have heard but one feeling expressed about [the Maryland campaign] and that is a regret at our having gone there. Our Army has shown itself incapable of invasion and we had better stick to the defensive." The Army of Northern Virginia's retreat across the Potomac ended a long series of Southern victories in the Eastern theater of the Civil War and dampened hopes for aid from Britain or France. During the first year and a half of the conflict, the outnumbered Confederacy had amassed high casualties in the East and West, suffered during its triumphs as well as its defeats. The carnage at Sharpsburg added to this gruesome accounting and contributed to the human attrition which eventually defeated the South.

The Union success in the Antietam campaign, limited as it was, gave President Lincoln his opportunity to issue the preliminary Emancipation Proclamation. The chief executive had read a draft of this document to his cabinet late in July, but they had persuaded him that if he announced the policy then, while the government's war effort seemed to be going so badly, it would appear to be a cry of desperation. A few days after Lee's retreat, Lincoln seized his chance to send the newspapers his statement of the war's new purpose. His preliminary Emancipation Proclamation stated that on January 1, 1863, all slaves in any state or district still in rebellion against the United States "shall be then, thenceforward, and forever free."

The traumatic battle which took place in the Antietam valley was one of the most memorable in American history. The dramatic story of Robert E. Lee's desperate stand in front of Sharpsburg and George B. McClellan's indecisive yet bloody attacks across the rolling hills gained a lasting place in the nation's memory. Northerners and Southerners alike admired Clara Barton's devoted aid to the maimed and dying soldiers and recognized the Antietam battlefield as the birthplace of the American Red Cross. The tragic battle in Maryland also was tied in the nation's memory to Abraham Lincoln's noble proclamation of the end of slavery.

The fields around Sharpsburg became a national monument to the courage of the common soldiers of the North and South. On Memorial Day 1885 at the Antietam National Cemetery, General McClellan addressed a crowd of veterans not only from the Army of the Potomac but also from the Army of Northern Virginia. Dressed in a faded blue uniform, the same one he had worn on the day of the battle, the old soldier spoke proudly of the bravery of his own men, and of their opponents.

Many in the audience at the cemetery that day could remember seeing the dawn of September 17, 1862. They recalled hearing the long roll of the drums through the morning fog. Frightened but determined, they had picked up their rifles and endured the bloodiest single day in American history.

Note: The Tables of Organization presented in Appendices A and B are taken from *War of the Rebellion: Official Records of the Union and Confederate Armies*, republished by The National Historical Society, 1972.

# APPENDIX A

# ORGANIZATION OF THE ARMY OF THE POTOMAC

## COMMANDER

MAJ. GEN. GEORGE B. MCCLELLAN [1]

### *GENERAL HEADQUARTERS*

ESCORT

CAPT. JAMES B. MCINTYRE

Independent Company Oneida (New York) Cavalry,
Capt. Daniel P. Mann

4th U.S. Cavalry, Company A, Lieut. Thomas H. McCormick

4th U.S. Cavalry, Company E, Capt. James B. McIntyre

VOLUNTEER ENGINEERING BRIGADE [2]

BRIG. GEN. DANIEL P. WOODBURY

15th New York, Col. John McL. Murphy

50th New York, Lieut. Col. William H. Pettes

REGULAR ENGINEERING BATTALION

CAPT. JAMES C. DUANE

PROVOST GUARD [3]

MAJ. WILLIAM H. WOOD

2d U.S. Cavalry, Companies E, F, H, and K, Capt. George A. Gordon

8th U.S. Infantry, Companies A, D, F, and G, Capt. Royal T. Frank

19th U.S. Infantry, Company G, Capt. Edmund L. Smith

19th U.S. Infantry, Company H, Capt. Henry S. Welton

---

[1] On September 14 the right wing of the army, consisting of the First and Ninth Corps, was commanded by Major-General Burnside; the center composed of the Second and Twelfth Corps, by Major-General Sumner; and the left wing, comprising the Sixth Corps and Couch's division (Fourth Corps), by Major-General Franklin.

[2] Detached at Washington, D.C., since September 7.

[3] The composition of this command is not fully reported on the returns.

HEADQUARTERS GUARD
MAJ. GRANVILLE O. HALLER

Sturges (Illinois) Rifles, Capt. James Steel [4]
93d New York, Lieut. Col. Benjamin C. Butler

QUARTERMASTER'S GUARD
1st U.S. Cavalry, Companies B, C, H, and I, Capt. Marcus A. Reno

## FIRST ARMY CORPS [5]
MAJ. GEN. JOSEPH HOOKER [6]
BRIG. GEN. George G. Meade

ESCORT
2nd New York Cavalry, Companies A, B, I, and K, Capt. John E. Naylor

FIRST DIVISION
BRIG. GEN. RUFUS KING [7]
BRIG. GEN. JOHN P. HATCH [8]
BRIG. GEN. ABNER DOUBLEDAY

*First Brigade*
COL. WALTER PHELPS, JR.

22d New York, Lieut. Col. John McKie, Jr.
24th New York, Capt. John D. O'Brian
30th New York, Col. William M. Searing
84th New York (14th Militia), Maj. William H. deBevoise
2d U.S. Sharpshooters, Col. Henry A.V. Post

*Second Brigade*
BRIG. GEN. ABNER DOUBLEDAY
COL. WILLIAM P. WAINWRIGHT [6]

LIEUT. COL. J. WILLIAM HOFMANN

7th Indiana, Maj. Ira G. Grover
76th New York, Col. William P. Wainwright, Capt. John W. Young
95th New York, Maj. Edward Pye
56th Pennsylvania, Lieut. Col. J. William Hofmann,
   Capt. Frederick Williams

[4] Detached at Washington, D.C., since September 7.
[5] Designation change from Third Corps, Army of Virginia, to First Army Corps by General
   Orders, No. 129, Adjutant-General's Office, September 12, 1862.
[6] Wounded September 17.
[7] Relieved September 14.
[8] Wounded September 14.

*Third Brigade*
BRIG. GEN. MARSENA R. PATRICK

21st New York, Col. William F. Rogers
23rd New York, Col. Henry C. Hoffman
35th New York, Col. Newton B. Lord
80th New York, (20th Militia), Lieut. Col. Theodore B. Gates

*Fourth Brigade*
BRIG. GEN. JOHN GIBBON

19th Indiana, Col. Solomon Meredith, Lieut. Col. Alois O. Bachman,
Capt. William W. Dudley
2d Wisconsin, Col. Lucius Fairchild, Lieut. Col. Thomas S. Allen
6th Wisconsin, Lieut. Col. Edward S. Bragg, Maj. Rufus R. Dawes
7th Wisconsin, Capt. John B. Callis

*Artillery*
CAPT. J. ALBERT MONROE

New Hampshire Light, First Battery, Lieut. Federick M. Edgell
1st Rhode Island Light, Battery D, Capt. J. Albert Monroe
1st New York Light, Battery L, Capt. John A. Reynolds
4th United States Battery B, Capt. Joseph B. Campbell,
    Lieut. James Stewart

SECOND DIVISION
BRIG. GEN. JAMES B. RICKETTS

*First Brigade*
BRIG. GEN. ABRAM DURYEA

97th New York, Maj. Charles Northrup
104th New York, Maj. Lewis C. Skinner
105th New York, Col. Howard Carroll
107th Pennsylvania, Capt. James Mac Thomson

*Second Brigade*
COL. WILLIAM A. CHRISTIAN
COL. PETER LYLE

26th New York, Lieut. Col. Richard H. Richardson
94th New York, Lieut. Col. Calvin Littlefield
88th Pennsylvania, Lieut. Col. George W. Gile, Capt. Henry R. Myers
90th Pennsylvania, Col. Peter Lyle, Lieut. Col. William A. Leech

*Third Brigade*
BRIG. GEN. GEORGE L. HARTSUFF [9]
COL. RICHARD COULTER

16th Maine [10], Col. Asa W. Wildes
12th Massachusetts, Maj. Elisha Burbank, Capt. Benjamin F. Cook
13th Massachusetts, Maj. J. Parker Gould
83d New York (9th Militia), Lieut. Col. William Atterbury
11th Pennsylvania, Col. Richard Coulter, Capt. David M. Cook

*Artillery*

1st Pennsylvania Light, Battery F, Capt. Ezra W. Matthews
Pennsylvania Light, Battery C, Capt. James Thompson

THIRD DIVISION
BRIG. GEN. GEORGE G. MEADE
BRIG. GEN. TRUMAN SEYMOUR

*First Brigade*
BRIG. GEN. TRUMAN SEYMOUR
COL. R. BIDDLE ROBERTS

1st Pennsylvania Reserves, Col. R. Biddle Roberts,
    Capt. William C. Talley
2d Pennsylvania Reserves, Capt. James N. Byrnes
5th Pennsylvania Reserves, Col. Joseph W. Fisher
6th Pennsylvania Reserves, Col. William Sinclair
13th Pennsylvania Reserves (1st Rifles), Col. Hugh W. McNeil,
    Capt. Dennis McGee

[9] Wounded September 17.
[10] Joined September 9, and detached September 13 as railroad guard.

*Second Brigade*
Col. Albert L. Magilton
3d Pennsylvania Reserves, Lieut. Col. John Clark
4th Pennsylvania Reserves, Maj. John Nyce
7th Pennsylvania Reserves, Col. Henry C. Bollinger, Maj.
Chauncey A. Lyman
8th Pennsylvania Reservges, Maj. Silas M. Baily

*Third Brigade*
Col. Thomas F. Gallagher [11]
Lieut. Col. Robert Anderson

9th Pennsylvania Reserves, Lieut. Col. Robert Anderson,
Capt. Samuel B. Dick
10th Pennsylvania Reserves, Lieut. Col. Adoniram J. Warner,
Capt. Jonathan P. Smith
11th Pennsylvania Reserves, Lieut. Col. Samuuel M. Jackson
12 Pennsylvania Reserves, Capt. Richard Gustin

*Artillery*

1st Pennsylvania Light, Battery A, Lieut. John G. Simpson
1st Pennsylvania Light, Battery B, Capt. James H. Cooper
1st Pennsylvania Light, Battery G [12], Lieut. Frank P. Amsden
5th United States, Battery C, Capt. Dunbar R. Ransom

**SECOND ARMY CORPS**
Maj. Gen. Edwin V. Sumner

ESCORT

6th New York Cavalry, Company D, Capt. Henry W. Lyon
6th New York Cavalry, Company K, Capt. Riley Johnson

FIRST DIVISION
Maj. Gen. Israel B. Richardson [13]
Brig. Gen. John C. Caldwell
Brig. Gen. Winfield S. Hancock

[11] Wounded September 14.
[12] Detached at Washington, D. C., since September 6.
[13] Wounded September 17.

*First Brigade*
BRIG. GEN. JOHN C. CALDWELL

5th New Hampshire, Col. Edward E. Cross
7th New York, Capt. Charles Brestel
61st New York, Col. Francis C. Barlow, Lieut. Col. Nelson A. Miles
64th New York, Col. Francis C. Barlow, Lieut. Col. Nelson A. Miles
81st Pennsylvania, Maj. H. Boyd McKeen

*Second Brigade*
BRIG. GEN. THOMAS F. MEAGHER
COL. JOHN BURKE

29th Massachusetts, Lieut. Col. Joseph H. Barnes
63d New York, Col. John Burke, Lieut. Col. Henry Fowler, Maj.
　Richard C. Bentley, Capt. Joseph O'Neill
69th New York, Lieut. Col. James Kelly, Maj. James Cavanagh
88th New York, Lieut. Col. Patrick Kelly

*Third Brigade*
COL. JOHN R. BROOKE

2d Delaware, Capt. David L. Stricker
52d New York, Col. Paul Frank
57th New York, Lieut. Col. Philip J. Parisen, Maj. Alford B. Chapman
66th New York, Capt. Julius Wehle, Lieut. Col. James H. Bull
53d Pennsylvania, Lieut. Col. Richards McMichael

*Artillery*

1st New York Light, Battery B, Capt. Rufus D. Pettit
4th United States Batteries, A and C, Lieut. Evan Thomas

SECOND DIVISION
MAJ. GEN. JOHN SEDGWICK [14]
BRIG. GEN. OLIVER O. HOWARD

---

[14] Wounded September 17.

*First Brigade*
BRIG. GEN. WILLIS A. GORMAN
15th Massachusetts, Lieut. Col. John W. Kimball
1st Minnesota, Col. Alfred Sully
34th New York, Col. James A. Suiter
82d New York, (2d Militia) Col. Henry W. Hudson
Massachusetts Sharpshooters, First Company, Capt. John Saunders
Minnesota Sharphooters, Second Company, Capt. William F. Russell

*Second Brigade*
BRIG. GEN. OLIVER O. HOWARD
COL. JOSHUA T. OWEN
COL. DEWITT C. BAXTER

69th Pennsylvania, Col. Joshua T. Owen
71st Pennsylvania, Col. Isaac J. Wistar, Lieut. Richard P. Smith
   (adjutant), Capt. Enoch E. Lewis
72d Pennsylvania, Col. DeWitt C. Baxter
106th Pennsylvania, Col. Turner G. Morhead

*Third Brigade*
BRIG. GEN. NAPOLEON J. T. DANA [15]
COL. NORMAN A. HALL

19th Massachusetts, Col. Edward W. Hinks, Lieut.
   Col. Arthur F. Devereux
20th Massachusetts, Col. William R. Lee
7th Michigan, Col. Norman J. Hall, Capt. Charles J. Hunt
42d New York, Lieut. Col. George N. Bomford, Maj. James E. Mallon
59th New York, Col. William L. Tidball

*Artillery*

1st Rhode Island Light, Battery A, Capt. John A. Tompkins
1st United States Battery I, Lieut. George A. Woodruff

THIRD DIVISION
BRIG. GEN. WILLIAM H. FRENCH

---

[15] Wounded September 17.

*First Brigade*

BRIG. GEN. NATHAN KIMBALL

14th Indiana, Col. William Harrow

8th Ohio, Lieut. Col. Franklin Sawyer

132d Pennsylvania, Col. Richard A. Oakford, Lieut.
Col. Vincent M. Wilcox

7th West Virginia, Col. Joseph Snider

*Second Brigade*

COL. DWIGHT MORRIS

14th Connecticut, Lieut. Col. Sanford H. Perkins

108th New York, Col. Oliver H. Palmer

130th Pennsylvania, Col. Henry I. Zinn

*Third Brigade*

BRIG. GEN. MAX WEBER [16]

COL. JOHN W. ANDREWS

1st Delaware, Col. John W. Andrews, Lieut. Col. Oliver Hopkinson

5th Maryland, Maj. Leopold Blumenberg, Capt. E.F.M. Faehtz

4th New York, Lieut. Col. John D. McGregor

UNATTACHED ARTILLERY

1st New York Light, Battery G, Capt. John D. Frank

1st Rhode Island Light, Battery B, Capt. John G. Hazard

1st Rhode Island Light, Battery G, Capt. Charles D. Owen

---

[16] Wounded September 17.

## FOURTH ARMY CORPS

### FIRST DIVISION [17]
#### MAJ. GEN. DARIUS N. COUCH

*First Brigade*
#### BRIG. GEN. CHARLES DEVENS, JR.

7th Massachusetts, Col. David A. Russell
10th Massachusetts, Col. Henry L. Eustis
36th New York, Col. William H. Browne
2d Rhode Island, Col. Frank Wheaton

*Second Brigade*
#### BRIG. GEN. ALBION P. HOWE

62d New York, Col. David J. Nevin
93d Pennsylvania, Col. James M. McCarter
98th Pennsylvania, Col. John F. Ballier
102d Pennsylvania, Col. Thomas A. Rowley
139th Pennsylvania, [18] Col. Frank H. Collier

*Third Brigade*
#### BRIG. GEN. JOHN COCHRANE

65th New York, Col. Alexandre Shaler
67th New York, Col. Julius W. Adams
122d New York, Col. Silas Titus
23d Pennsylvania, Col. Thomas H. Neill
61st Pennsylvania, Col. George C. Spear
82d Pennsylvania, Col. David H. Williams

*Artillery*

New York Light, Third Battery, Capt. William Stuart [19]
1st Pennsylvania Light, Battery C, Capt. Jeremiah McCarthy
1st Pennsylvania Light, Battery D, Capt. Michael Hall
2d United States, Battery G, Lieut. John H. Butler

[17] Assigned to the Sixth Corps as the Third Division September 26, 1862.
[18] Joined September 17.
[19] Joined September 15.

## FIFTH ARMY CORPS
### MAJ. GEN. FITZ JOHN PORTER

### ESCORT
1st Maine Cavalry (detachment), Capt. George B. Summat

### FIRST DIVISION
### MAJ. GEN. GEORGE W. MORELL

*First Brigade*
### COL. JAMES BARNES

2d Maine, Col. Charles W. Roberts
18th Massachusetts, Lieut.Col. Joseph Hayes
22d Massachusetts, Lieut.Col. William S. Tilton
1st Michigan, Capt. Emory W. Belton
13th New York, Col. Elisha G. Marshall
25th New York, Col. Charles A. Johnson
118th Pennsylvania, Col. Charles M. Prevost
Massachusetts Sharpshooters, Second Company,
    Capt. Lewis E. Wentworth

*Second Brigade*
### BRIG. GEN. CHARLES GRIFFIN

2d District of Columbia, Col. Charles M. Alexander
9th Massachusetts, Col. Patrick R. Guiney
32d Massachusetts, Col. Francis J. Parker
4th Michigan, Col. Jonathan W. Childs
14th New York, Col. James McQuade
62d Pennsylvania, Col. Jacob B. Sweitzer

*Third Brigade*
### COL. T. B. W. STOCKTON

20th Maine, Col. Adelbert Ames
16th Michigan, Lieut. Col. Norval E. Welch
12th New York, Capt. William Huson
17th New York. Lieut. Col. Nelson B. Bartram
44th New York, Maj. Freeman Conner
83d Pennsylvania, Capt. Orpheus S. Woodward
Michigan Sharpshooters, Brady's company, Lieut. Jonas H. Titus, Jr.

*Artillery*

Massachusetts Light, Battery C, Capt. Augustus P. Martin
1st Rhode Island Light, Battery C, Capt. Richard Waterman
5th United States, Battery D, Lieut. Charles E. Hazlett

*Sharpshooters*

1st United States, Capt. John B. Isler

SECOND DIVISION
BRIG. GEN. GEORGE SYKES

*First Brigade*
LIEUT. COL. ROBERT C. BUCHANAN

3d United States, Capt. John D. Wilkins
4th United States, Capt. Hiram Dryer
12th United States, First Battalion, Capt. Matthew M. Blunt
12th United States, Second Battalion, Capt. Thomas M. Anderson
14th United States, First Battalion, W. Harvey Brown
14th United States, Second Battalion, Capt. David B. McKibbin

*Second Brigade*
MAJ. CHARLES S. LOVELL

1st and 6th United States, Capt. Levi C. Bootes
2d and 10th United States, Capt. John S. Poland
11th United States, Capt. DeL. Floyd-Jones
17th United States, Maj. George L. Andrews

*Third Brigade*
COL. GOUVERNEUR K. WARREN

5th New York, Capt. Cleveland Winslow
10th New York, Lieut. Col. John W. Marshall

*Artillery*

1st United States, Batteries E and G, Lieut. Alanson M. Randol
5th United States, Battery I, Capt. Stephen H. Weed
5th United States, Battery K, Lieut. William E. Van Reed

THIRD DIVISION [20]
BRIG. GEN. ANDREW A. HUMPHREYS

*First Brigade*
BRIG. GEN. ERASTUS B. TYLER

91st Pennsylvania, Col. Edgar M. Gregory
126 Pennsylvania, Col. James G. Elder
129 Pennsylvania, Col. Jacob G. Frick
134th Pennsylvania, Col. Matthew S. Quay

*Second Brigade*
COL.  PETER H. ALLABACH

123d Pennsylvania, Col. John B. Clark
131st Pennsylvania, Lieut. Col. William B. Shaut
133d Pennsylvania, Col. Franklin B. Speakman
155th Pennsylvania, Col. Edward J. Allen

*Artillery*
CAPT. LUCIUS N. ROBINSON

1st New York  Light, Battery C, Capt. Almont Barnes
1st Ohio Light, Battery L, Capt. Lucius N. Robinson

ARTILLERY RESERVE [21]
LIEUT. COL.  WILLIAM HAYS

1st Battalion New York  Light, Battery A, Lieut. Bernhard Wever
1st Battalion New York  Light, Battery B, Lieut. Alfred von Kleiser
1st Battalion New York  Light, Battery C, Capt. Robert Langner
1st Battalion New York  Light, Battery D, Capt. Charles Kusserow
New York  Light, Fifth Battery, Capt. Elijah D. Taft
1st United States Battery K, Capt. William M. Graham
4th United States, Battery G, Lieut. Marcus P. Miller

---

[20] This division was organized September 12, and reached the battlefield September 18.
[21] Batteries detached from the reserve are embraced in the roster of the commands with which they served.

## SIXTH ARMY CORPS
### MAJ. GEN. WILLIAM B. FRANKLIN

### ESCORT
6th Pennsylvania Cavalry, Companies B and G, Capt. Henry P. Muirheid

### FIRST DIVISION
### MAJ. GEN. HENRY W. SLOCUM

*First Brigade*
### COL. ALFRED T.A. TORBERT

1st New Jersey, Lieut. Col. Mark W. Collet
2d New Jersey, Col. Samuel L. Buck
3d New Jersey, Col. Henry W. Brown
4th New Jersey, Col.William B. Hatch

*Second Brigade*
### COL. JOSEPH J. BARTLETT

5th Maine, Col. Nathaniel J. Jackson
16th New York, Lieut. Col. Joel J. Seaver
27th New York, Lieut. Col. Alexander D. Adams
96th Pennsylvania, Col. Henry L. Cake

*Third Brigade*
### BRIG. GEN. JOHN NEWTON

18th New York, Lieut. Col. George R. Myers
31st New York, Lieut. Col. Francis E. Pinto
32d New York, Col. Roderick Matheson, Maj. George F. Lemon
95th Pennsylvania, Col. Gustavus W. Town

*Artillery*
### CAPT. EMORY UPTON

Maryland Light, Battery A, Capt. John W. Wolcott
Massachusetts Light, Battery A, Capt. Josiah Porter
New Jersey Light, Battery A, Capt. William Hexamer
2d United States, Battery D, Lieut. Edward B. Williston

SECOND DIVISION
MAJ. GEN. WILLIAM F. SMITH

*First Brigade*
BRIG. GEN. WINFIELD S. HANCOCK [22]
COL. AMASA COBB

6th Maine, Col. Hiram Burnham
43d New York , Maj. John Wilson
49th Pennsylvania, Lieut. Col. William Brisbane
137th Pennsylvania, Col. Henry M. Bossert
5th Wisconsin, Col. Amasa Cobb

*Second Brigade*
BRIG. GEN. W .T .H. BROOKS

2d Vermont, Maj. James H. Walbridge
3d Vermont, Col. Breed N. Hyde
4th Vermont, Lieut. Col. Charles B. Stoughton
5th Vermont, Col. Lewis A. Grant
6th Vermont, Maj. Oscar L. Tuttle

*Third Brigade*
COL. WILLIAM H. IRWIN

7th Maine, Maj. Thomas W. Hyde
20th New York, Col. Ernest von Vegesack
33d New York, Lieut. Col. Joseph W. Corning
49th New York, Lieut. Col. William C. Alberger,
    Maj. George W. Johnson
77th New York, Capt. Nathan S. Babcock

*Artillery* [23]
CAPT. ROMEYN B. AYRES

Maryland Light, Battery B, Lieut. Theodore J. Vanneman
New York  Light, 1st Battery, Capt. Andrew Cowan
5th United States, Battery F, Lieut. Leonard Martin

---

[22] Assigned to command the First Division, Second Army Corps, September 17.
[23] The Third Battery New York Light Artillery transferred to Couch's division September 15.

## NINTH ARMY CORPS
MAJ. GEN. AMBROSE E. BURNSIDE [24]
MAJ. GEN. JESSE L. RENO [25]
BRIG. GEN. JACOB D. COX

ESCORT
1st Maine Cavalry, Company G, Capt. Zebulon B. Blethen

FIRST DIVISION
BRIG, GEN. ORLANDO B. WILLCOX

*First Brigade*
COL. BENJAMIN C. CHRIST

28th Massachusetts, Capt. Andrew P. Caraher
17th Michigan, Col. William H. Withington
79th New York , Lieut. Col. David Morrison
50th Pennsylvania, Maj. Edward Overton, Capt. William H. Diehl

*Second Brigade*
COL. THOMAS WELSH

8th Michigan[26], Lieut. Col. Frank Graves, Maj. Ralph Ely
46th New York , Lieut. Col. Joseph Gerhardt
45th Pennsylvania, Lieut. Col. John I. Curtin
100th Pennsylvania, Lieut. Col. David A. Leckey

*Artillery*

Massachusetts Light, Eighth Battery, Capt. Asa M. Cook
2d United States, Battery E. Lieut. Samuel N. Benjamin

SECOND DIVISION
BRIG. GEN. SAMUEL D. STURGIS

[24] On the 16th and 17th Major-General Burnside exercised general command on the left and Brigadier-General Cox was in immediate command of the corps.
[25] Killed September 14.
[26] Transferred from First Brigade September 16.

*First Brigade*
BRIG. GEN. JAMES NAGLE

2d Maryland, Lieut. Col. J. Eugene Duryea
6th New Hampshire, Col. Simon G. Griffin
9th New Hampshire, Col. Enoch Q. Fellows
48th Pennsylvania, Lieut. Col. Joshua K. Sigfried

*Second Brigade*
BRIG. GEN. EDWARD FERRERO

21st Massachusetts, Col. William S. Clark
35th Massachusetts, Col. Edward A. Wild, Lieut.
  Col. Sumner Carruth
51st New York, Col. Robert B. Potter
51st Pennsylvania, Col. John F. Hartranft

*Artillery*

Pennsylvania Light, Battery D, Capt. Goerge W. Durell
4th United States, Battery E, Capt. Joseph C. Clark, Jr.

THIRD DIVISION
BRIG. GEN ISAAC P. RODMAN [27]

*First Brigade*
COL. HARRISON S. FAIRCHILD

9th New York, Lieut. Col. Edgar A. Kimball
89th New York, Maj. Edward Jardine
103d New York, Maj. Benjamin Ringold

*Second Brigade*
COL. EDWARD HARLAND

8th Connecticut, Lieut. Col. Hiram Appelman, Maj. John E. Ward
11th Connecticut, Col. Henry W. Kingsbury
16th Connecticut, Col. Francis Beach[28]
4th Rhode Island, Col. William H. P. Steere, Lieut.
  Col. Joseph B. Curtis

[27] Wounded September 17.
[28] Assigned September 16.

*Artillery*

5th United States, Battery A, Lieut. Charles P. Muhlenberg

## KANAWHA DIVISION
### BRIG. GEN. JACOB D. COX
### COL. ELIAKIM P. SCAMMON

*First Brigade*
### COL. ELIAKIM P. SCAMMON
### COL. HUGH EWING

12th Ohio, Col. Carr B. White
23d Ohio, Lieut. Col. Rutherford B. Hayes, Maj. James M. Comly
30th Ohio, Col. Hugh Ewing, Lieut. Col. Theodore Jones,
    Maj. George H. Hildt
Ohio Light Artillery, First Battery, Capt. James R. McMullin
Gilmore's company West Virginia Cavalry, Lieut. James Abraham
Harrison's company West Virginia Cavalry, Lieut. Dennis Delaney

*Second Brigade*
### COL. GEORGE CROOK

11th Ohio, Lieut. Col. Augustus H. Coleman, Maj. Lyman J. Jackson
28th Ohio, Lieut. Col. Gottfried Becker
36th Ohio, Lieut. Col. Melvin Clarke
Schambeck's company Chicago Dragoons, Capt. Frederick Shambeck
Kentucky Light Artillery, Simmonds battery, Capt. Seth J. Simmonds

### UNATTACHED

6th New York Cavalry (eight companies), Col. Thomas C. Devin
Ohio Cavalry, Third Independent Company, Lieut. Jonas Seamen
3d U.S. Artillery, Batteries L and M, Capt. John Edwards, Jr.

## TWELFTH ARMY CORPS [29]
### MAJ. GEN. JOSEPH K. F. MANSFIELD [30]
### BRIG. GEN. ALPHEUS S. WILLIAMS

---

[29] Designation changed from Second Corps, Army of Virginia, to Twelfth Army Corps, by
General Orders, No. 129, Adjutant-General's Office, September 12, 1862.
[30] Mortally wounded September 17.

ESCORT

1st Michigan Cavalry, Company L, Capt. Melvin Brewer

FIRST DIVISION

BRIG. GEN. ALPHEUS S. WILLIAMS

BRIG. GENERAL SAMUEL W. CRAWFORD [31]

BRIG. GEN. GEORGE H. GORDON

*First Brigade*

BRIG. GEN. SAMUEL W. CRAWFORD

COL. JOSEPH F. KNIPE

5th Connecticut, Capt. Henry W. Daboll [32]

10th Maine, Col. George L. Beal

28th New York, Capt. William H. H. Mapes

46th Pennsylvania, Col. Joseph F. Knipe, Lieut.
Col. James L. Selfridge

124th Pennsylvania, Col. Joseph W. Hawley, Maj. Isaac L. Haldeman

125th Pennsylvania, Col. Jacob Higgins

128th Pennsylvania, Col. Samuel Croasdale, Lieut.
Col. William W. Hammersly, Maj. Joel B. Wanner

*Third Brigade*

BRIG. GEN. GEORGE H. GORDON

COL. THOMAS H. RUGER

27th Indiana, Col. Silas Colgrove

2d Massachusetts, Col. George L. Andrews

13th New Jersey, Col. Ezra A. Carman

107th New York, Col. R. B. Van Valkenburgh

Zouaves d'Afrique, Pennsylvania [33]

3d Wisconsin, Col. Thomas H. Ruger

SECOND DIVISION

BRIG. GEN. GEORGE S. GREENE

---

[31] Wounded September 17.

[32] Detached at Frederick, Md., since September 15.

[33] No officers present; enlisted men of company attached to Second Massachusetts.

*First Brigade*
LIEUT. COL. HECTOR TYNDALE [34]
MAJ. ORRIN J. CRANE

5th Ohio, Maj. John Collins
7th Ohio, Maj. Orrin J. Crane, Capt. Frederick A. Seymour
29th Ohio [35], Lieut. Theron S. Winship
66th Ohio, Lieut. Col. Eugene Powell
28th Pennsylvania, Maj. Ario Pardee, Jr.

*Second Brigade*
COL. HENRY J. STAINROOK

3d Maryland, Lieut. Col. Joseph M. Sudsburg
102d New York, Lieut. Col. James C. Lane
109th Pennsylvania [36], Capt. George E. Seymour
111th Pennsylvania, Maj. Thomas M. Walker

*Third Brigade*
COL. WILLIAM B. GOODRICH [37]
LIEUT. COL. JONATHAN AUSTIN

3d Delaware, Maj. Arthur Maginnis
Purnell Legion, Maryland, Lieut. Col. Benjamin L. Simpson
60th New York, Col. Charles R. Brundage
78th New York, Lieut. Col. Jonathan Austin, Capt. Henry R. Stagg

ARTILLERY
CAPT. CLERMONT L. BEST

Maine Light, 4th Battery, Capt. O'Neil W. Robinson
Maine Light, 6th Battery, Capt. Freeman McGilvery
1st New York Light, Battery M, Capt. George W. Cothran
New York Light, 10th Battery, Capt. John T. Bruen
Pennsylvania Light, Battery E, Capt. Joseph M. Knap
Pennsylvania Light, Battery F, Capt. Robert B. Hampton
4th United States, Battery F, Lieut. Edward D. Muhlenberg

CAVALRY DIVISION
BRIG. GEN. ALFRED PLEASONTON

[34] Wounded September 17.
[35] Detached September 9.
[36] Detached September 13.
[37] Killed September 17.

*First Brigade*
MAJ. CHARLES W. WHITING
5th United States, Capt. Joseph H. McArthur
6th United States, Capt. William P. Sanders

*Second Brigade*
COL. JOHN F. FARNSWORTH

8th Illinois, Maj. William H. Medill
3d Indiana, Maj. George H. Chapman
1st Massachusetts, Capt. Casper Crowninshield
8th Pennsylvania [38], Capt. Peter Keenan

*Third Brigade*
COL. RICHARD H. RUSH

4th Pennsylvania, Col. James H. Childs, Lieut. Col. James K. Kerr
6th Pennsylvania, Lieut. Col. C. Ross Smith

*Fourth Brigade*
COL. ANDREW T. MCREYNOLDS

1st New York, Maj. Alonzo W. Adams
12th Pennsylvania, Maj. James A. Congdon

*Fifth Brigade*
COL. BENJAMIN F. DAVIS

8th New York, Col. Benjamin F. Davis
3d Pennsylvania, Lieut. Col. Samuel W. Owen

*Artillery*

2d United States, Battery A, Capt. John C. Tidball
2d United States, Batteries B and L, Capt. James M. Robertson
2d United States, Battery M, Lieut. Peter C. Hains
3d United States, Batteries C and G, Capt. Horatio G. Gibson

*Unattached*

1st Maine Cavalry, Col. Samuel H. Allen
15th Pennsylvania Cavalry, (detachment) Col. William J. Palmer

[38] Detached at Frederick, Md.

## APPENDIX B

## ORGANIZATION OF THE ARMY OF NORTHERN VIRGINIA

### COMMANDER
GEN. ROBERT E. LEE

### LONGSTREET'S CORPS
MAJ. GEN. JAMES LONGSTREET

#### MCLAWS' DIVISION
MAJ. GEN. LAFAYETTE MCLAWS

*Kershaw's Brigade*
BRIG. GEN. J. B. KERSHAW

2d South Carolina, Col. John D. Kennedy
3d South Carolina, Col. James D. Nance
7th South Carolina, Col. D. Wyatt Aiken, Capt. John S. Hard
8th South Carolina, Lieut. Col. A.J. Hoole

*Cobb's Brigade*
BRIG. GEN. HOWELL COBB
LIEUT. COL. C.C. SANDERS
LIEUT. COL. WILLIAM MACRAE

16th Georgia
24th Georgia
Cobb's (Georgia) Legion
15th North Carolina

*Semmes' Brigade*
BRIG. GEN. PAUL J. SEMMES

10th Georgia, Capt. P.H. Loud
53d Georgia, Lieut. Col. Thomas Sloan, Capt. S.W. Marshborne
15th Virginia, Capt. E.M. Morrison and Capt. E.J. Willis
32d Virginia, Col. E.B. Montague

*Barksdale's Brigade*
BRIG. GEN. WILLIAM BARKSDALE

13th Mississippi, Lieut. Col. Kennon McElroy
17th Mississippi, Lieut. Col. John C. Fiser
18th Mississippi, Maj. J.C. Campbell, Lieut. Col. William H. Luse
21st Mississippi, Capt. John Sims, Col. Benjamin G. Humphreys

*Artillery*
MAJ. S.P. HAMILTON
COL. H.C. CABELL

Manly's (North Carolina) Battery, Capt. B.C. Manly
Pulaski (Georgia) Artillery, Capt. J.P.W. Read
Richmond (Fayette) Artillery, Capt. M.C. Macon
Richmond Howitzers, (1st company), Capt. E.S. McCarthy
Troup (Georgia) Artillery, Capt. H.H. Carlton

ANDERSON'S DIVISION
MAJ. GEN. RICHARD H. ANDERSON

*Wilcox's Brigade*
COL. ALFRED CUMMING

8th Alabama
9th Alabama
10th Alabama
11th Alabama

*Mahone's Brigade*
COL. WILLIAM A. PARHAM

6th Virginia
12th Virginia
16th Virginia
41st Virginia
61st Virginia

*Featherston's Brigade*
BRIG. GEN. WINFIELD S. FEATHERSTON
COL. CARNOT POSEY

12th Mississippi
16th Mississippi, Capt. A.M. Feltus
19th Mississippi
2d Mississippi Battalion

*Armistead's Brigade*
BRIG. GEN. LEWIS A. AMISTEAD
COL. J.G. HODGES

9th Virginia
14th Virginia
38th Virginia
53d Virginia
57th Virginia

*Pryor's Brigade*
BRIG. GEN. ROGER A. PRYOR

14th Alabama
2d Florida
8th Florida
3d Virginia

*Wright's Brigade*
BRIG. GEN. A.R. WRIGHT

44th Alabama
3d Georgia
22d Georgia
48th Georgia

*Artillery*
MAJ. JOHN S. SAUNDERS

Donaldsonville (Louisiana) Artillery (Maurin's Battery)
Huger's (Virginia) Battery
Moorman's (Virginia) Battery
Thompson's (Grimes') (Virginia) Battery

JONES' DIVISION
BRIG. GEN. DAVID R. JONES

*Toomb's Brigade*
BRIG. GEN. ROBERT TOOMBS
COL. HENRY L. BENNING

2d Georgia, Lieut. Col. William R. Holmes, Maj. Skidmore Harris
15th Georgia, Col. W.T. Millican
17th Georgia, Capt. J.A. McGregor
20 Georgia, Col. J.B. Cumming

*Drayton's Brigade*
BRIG. GEN. THOMAS F. DRAYTON

50th Georgia, Lieut. Col. F. Kearse
51st Georgia
15th South Carolina, Col. W.D. DeSaussure

*Pickett's Brigade*
COL. EPPA HUNTON
BRIG. GEN. R.B. GARNETT

8th Virginia, Col. Eppa Hunton
18th Virginia, Maj. George C. Cabell
19th Virginia, Col. J.B. Strange, Lieut. W.N. Wood, Capt. J.L. Cochran
28th Virginia, Capt. Wingfield
56th Virginia, Col. William D. Stuart and Capt. McPhail

*Kemper's Brigade*
BRIG. GEN. J.L. KEMPER

1st Virginia
7th Virginia
11th Virginia
17th Virginia
24th Virginia

*Jenkin's Brigade*
COL. JOSEPH WALKER

1st South Carolina (Volunteers), Lieut. Col. D. Livingston
2d South Carolina Rifles
5th South Carolina, Capt. T.C. Beckham
6th South Carolina, Lieut. Col. J.M. Steedman, Capt. E.B. Cantey
4th South Carolina Battalion
Palmetto (South Carolina) Sharpshooters

*Anderson's Brigade*
COL. GEORGE T. ANDERSON

1st Georgia (Regulars), Col. W.J. Magill
7th Georgia
8th Georgia
9th Georgia
11th Georgia, Maj. F.H. Little

*Artillery*

Fauquier (Virginia) Artillery (Stribling's Battery)[1]
Loudoun (Virginia) Artillery (Rogers" Battery) [1]
Turner (Virginia) Artillery (Leake's Battery) [1]
Wise (Virginia) Artillery (J.S. Brown's Battery)

WALKER'S DIVISION
BRIG. GEN. JOHN G. WALKER

*Walker's Brigade*
COL. VAN H. MANNING
COL. E.D. HALL

3d Arkansas, Capt. John W. Reedy
27th North Carolina, Col. J.R. Cook
46th North Carolina, Col. E.D. Hall
48th North Carolina, Col. R.C. Hill
30th Virginia
French's (Virginia) battery, Capt. Thomas B. French

[1] Left at Leesburg.

*Ransom's Brigade*
BRIG. GEN. ROBERT RANSOM JR.

24th North Carolina, Lieut. Col. John L. Harris
25th North Carolina, Col. H.M. Rutledge
35th North Carolina, Col. M.W. Ransom
49th North Carolina, Lieut. Col. Lee M. McAfee
Branch's Field Artillery (Virginia), Capt. Branch

HOOD'S DIVISION
BRIG. GEN. JOHN B. HOOD

*Hood's Brigade*
COL. W.T. WOFFORD

18th Georgia, Lieut. Col. S.Z. Ruff
Hampton (South Carolina) Legion, Lieut. Col. M.W. Gary
1st Texas, Lieut. Col. P.A. Work
4th Texas, Lieut. Col. B.F. Carter
5th Texas, Capt. I.N.M. Turner

*Law's Brigade*
COL. E.M. LAW

4th Alabama, Lieut. Col. O.K. McLemore
2d Mississippi, Col. J.M. Stone
11th Mississippi, Col. P.F. Liddell
6th North Carolina, Maj. Robert F. Webb

*Artillery*
MAJ. B.W. FROBEL

German Artillery (South Carolina), Capt. W.K. Bachman
Palmetto Artillery (South Carolina), Capt. H.R. Garden
Rowan Artillery (North Carolina), Capt. James Reilly

*EVANS' BRIGADE*
BRIG. GEN. NATHAN G. EVANS
COL. P.F. STEVENS [2]

17 South Carolina, Col. F.W. McMaster
18th South Carolina, Col. W.H. Wallace
22d South Carolina, Lieut. Col. T.C. Watkins, Maj. M. Hilton
23d South Carolina, Capt. S.A. Durham, Lieut. E.R. White
Holcombe (South Carolina) Legion, Col. P.F. Stevens
Macbeth (South Carolina) Artillery, Capt. R. Boyce

ARTILLERY

WASHINGTON (LOUISIANA) ARTILLERY
COL. J.B. WALTON

1st Company, Capt. C.W. Squires
2d Company, Capt. J.B. Richardson
3d Company, Capt. M.B. Miller
4th Company, Capt. B.F. Eshleman

*Lee's Battalion*
COL. S.D. LEE

Ashland (Virginia) Artillery, Capt. P. Woolfolk, Jr.
Bedford (Virginia) Artillery, Capt. T.C. Jordan
Brooks (South Carolina) Artillery, Lieut. William Elliott
Eubank's (Virginia) Battery, J.L. Eubank
Madison (Louisiana) Light Artillery, Capt. G.V. Moody
Parker's (Virginia) Battery, Capt. W.W. Parker

**JACKSON'S CORPS**
MAJ. GEN. THOMAS J. JACKSON

EWELL'S DIVISION
BRIG. GEN. A.R. LAWTON
BRIG. GEN. JUBAL A. EARLY

[2] Commanding brigade while General Evans commanded provisional division.

*Lawton's Brigade*
COL. M. DOUGLASS
MAJ. J.H. LOWE
COL. JOHN H. LAMAR

13th Georgia
26th Georgia
31st Georgia, Lieut. Col. J.T. Crowder
38th Georgia
60th Georgia
61st Georgia

*Early's Brigade*
BRIG. GEN. JUBAL A. EARLY
COL. WILLIAM SMITH

13th Virginia, Capt. F.V. Winston
25th Virginia
31st Virginia
44th Virginia
49th Virginia, Col. William Smith
52d Virginia, Col. M.G. Harman
58th Virginia

*Trimble's Brigade*
COL. JAMES A. WALKER

15th Alabama, Capt. I.B. Feagin
12th Georgia, Capt. Rodgers
21st Georgia, Maj. Thomas C. Glover
21st North Carolina, Capt. Miller
1st North Carolina Battalion [3]

*Hays' Brigade*
BRIG. GEN. HARRY T. HAYS

5th Louisiana
6th Louisiana, Col. H.B. Strong
7th Louisiana
8th Louisiana
14th Louisiana

[3] Attached to Twenty-first North Carolina Regiment.

*Artillery* [4]

MAJ. A.R. COURTNEY

Charlottesville (Virginia) Artillery (Carrington's Battery)
Chesapeake (Maryland) Artillery (Brown's Battery)
Courtney (Virginia) Artillery (Latimer's Battery)
Johnson's (Virginia) Battery
Louisiana Guard Artillery (D'Aquin's Battery)
First Maryland battery (Dement's Battery)
Staunton (Virginia) Artillery (Balthis' Battery)

HILL'S LIGHT DIVISION
MAJ. GEN. AMBROSE P. HILL

*Branch's Brigade*
BRIG. GEN L. O'B. BRANCH
COL. JAMES H. LANE

7th North Carolina
18th North Carolina, Lieut. Col. Purdie
28th North Carolina
33d North Carolina
37th North Carolina

*Gregg's Brigade*
BRIG. GEN. MAXCY GREGG

1st South Carolina (Provisional Army), Maj. E. McCrady, Jr.,
Col. D.H. Hamilton
1st South Carolina Rifles, Lieut. Col. James M. Perrin
12th South Carolina, Col. Dixon Barnes, Lieut. Col. C. Jones,
Maj. W.H. McCorkle
13th South Carolina, Col. O.E. Edwards
14 South Carolina, Lieut. Col. W.D. Simpson

*Field's Brigade*
COL. J.M. BROCKEMBROUGH

40th Virginia
47th Virginia
55th Virginia
22d Virginia Battalion

[4] The Charlottesville Artillery, left at Richmond in August, did not rejoin the Army until after the battle of Sharpsburg. John R. Johnson's and D'Aquin's batteries were the only ones present with this division at Sharpsburg, the others having been left at Harper's Ferry and Shepherdstown.

*Archer's Brigade*
BRIG, GEN. J.J. ARCHER
COL. PETER TURNEY

5th Alabama Battalion, Capt. Hooper
19th Georgia, Maj. J.H. Neal, Capt. F.M. Johnston
1st Tennessee (Provisional Army) Col. Peter Turney
7th Tennessee, Maj. S.G. Shepard, Lieut. G.A. Howard
14th Tennessee, Lieut. Col. J.W. Lockert

*Pender's Brigade*
BRIG. GEN. WILLIAM D. PENDER
COL. R.H. BREWER

16th North Carolina, Lieut. Col. Stowe
22d North Carolina, Maj. C.C. Cole
34th North Carolina
38th North Carolina

*Thomas's Brigade*
COL. EDWARD L. THOMAS

14th Georgia, Col. R.W. Folsom
35th Georgia
45th Georgia, Maj. W.L. Grice
49th Georgia, Lieut. Col. S.M. Manning

*Artillery* [5]
MAJ. R.L. WALKER

Branch (North Carolina) Artillery (A.C. Latham's Battery)
Crenshaw's (Virginia) Battery
Fredericksburg (Virginia) Artillery (Braxton's Battery)
Letcher (Virginia) Artillery (Davidson's Battery)
Middlesex (Virginia) Artillery (Fleet's Battery)
Pee Dee (South Carolina) Artillery (McIntosh's Battery)
Purcell (Virginia) Artillery (Pegram's Battery)

---

[5] Braxton's, Crenshaw's, McIntosh's, and Pegram's batteries engaged at Sharpsburg. Davidson's battery had been left at Harper's Ferry, and Fleet's and Latham's batteries at Leesburg.

JACKSON'S DIVISION
BRIG. GEN. JOHN R. JONES
BRIG. GEN. W.E. STARKE
COL. A.J. GRIGSBY

*Winder's Brigade*
COL. A.J. GRIGSBY
LIEUT. COL. R.D. GARDNER (FOURTH VIRGINIA)
MAJ. H.J. WILLIAMS

2d Virginia, Capt. R.T. Colston
4th Virginia, Lieut. Col. R.D. Gardner
5th Virginia, Maj. H.J. Williams
27th Virginia, Capt. F.C. Wilson
33d Virginia, Capt. Golladay, Lieut. Walton

*Taliaferro's Brigade*
COL. E.T.H. WARREN
COL. J.W. JACKSON
COL. J.L. SHEFFIELD

47th Alabama
48th Alabama
10th Virginia
23d Virginia
37th Virginia

*Jones' Brigade*
COL. B.T. JOHNSON
BRIG. GEN. J.R. JONES
CAPT. J.E. PENN
CAPT. A.C. PAGE
CAPT. R.W. WITHERS

21st Virginia, Capt. A.C. Page
42d Virginia, Capt. R.W. Withers
48th Virginia, Capt. Chandler
1st Virginia Battalion, Lieut. C.A. Davidson

*Starke's Brigade*
BRIG. GEN. WILLIAM E. STARKE
COL. L.A. STAFFORD
COL. E. PENDLETON

1st Louisiana, Lieut. Col. M. Nolan
2d Louisiana, Col. J.M. Williams
9th Louisiana
10th Louisiana, Capt. H.D. Monier
15th Louisiana
Coppens' (Louisiana) Battalion

*Artillery*
MAJ. L.M. SHUMAKER

Alleghany (Virginia) Artillery (Carpenter's Battery)
Brockenbrough's (Maryland) Battery
Danville (Virginia) Artillery (Wooding's Battery)
Hampden (Virginia) Artillery (Caskie's Battery)
Lee (Virginia) Battery (Raine's Battery)
Rockbridge (Virginia) Artillery (Poague's Battery)

HILL'S DIVISION [6]
MAJ. GEN. DANIEL H. HILL

*Ripley's Brigade*
BRIG. GEN. ROSWELL S. RIPLEY
COL. GEORGE DOLES

4tth Georgia, Col. George Doles
44th Georgia, Capt. Key
1st North Carolina, Lieut. Col. H.A. Brown
3d North Carolina, Col. William L. DeRosset

*Rodes' Brigade*
BRIG. GEN. R.E. RODES

3d Alabama, Col. C.A. Battle
5th Alabama, Maj. E.L. Hobson
6th Alabama, Col. J.S. Gordon
12th Alabama, Col. B.B. Gayle, Lieut. Col. S.B. Pickens
26th Alabama, Col. E.A. O'Neal

[6] On "field return," Army of Northern Virginia, for September 22, this division appears as of Jackson's Corps.

*Garland's Brigade*
BRIG. GEN. SAMUEL GARLAND, JR.
COL. D.K. MCRAE

5th North Carolina, Col. D.K. McRae, Capt. T.M. Garrett
12th North Carolina, Capt. S. Snow
13th North Carolina, Lieut. Col. Thomas Ruffin, Jr.
20th North Carolina, Col. Alfred Iverson
23d North Carolina, Col. D.H. Christie

*Anderson's Brigade*
BRIG. GEN. GEORGE B. ANDERSON
COL. R.T. BENNETT

2d North Carolina, Col. C.C. Tew, Capt. G.M. Roberts
4th North Carolina, Col. Bryan Grimes, Capt. W.T. Marsh,
    Capt. D.P. Latham
14th North Carolina, Col. R.T. Bennett
30th North Carolina, Col. F.M. Parker, Maj. W.W. Sillers

*Colquitt's Brigade*
COL. A.H. COLQUITT

13th Alabama, Col. B.D. Fry
6th Georgia, Lieut. Col. J.M. Newton
23d Georgia, Col. W.P. Barclay
27th Georgia, Col. L.B. Smith
28th Georgia, Maj. T. Graybill, Capt. N.J. Garrison

*Artillery* [7]
MAJ. PIERSON

Hardaway's (Alabama) battery, Capt. R.A. Hardaway
Jeff Davis (Alabama) Artillery, Capt. J.W. Bondurant
Jones (Virginia) battery, Capt. William B. Jones
King William (Virginia) Artillery, Capt. T.H. Carter

[7] Cutt's and Jones' battalions also under D.H. Hill's command at Sharpsburg.

RESERVE ARTILLERY [8]
BRIG. GEN. WILLIAM N. PENDLETON

*Brown's Battalion* [9]
COL. J. THOMPSON BROWN

Powhatan Artillery (Dance's Battery)
Richmond Howitzers, 2d company (Watson's Battery)
Richmond Howitzers, 3d company (Smith's Battery)
Salem Artillery (Hupp's Battery)
Williamsburg Artillery (Coke's Battery)

*Cutt's Battalion* [10]
LIEUT. COL. A.S. CUTTS

Blackshears' (Georgia) Battery
Irwin (Georgia) Artillery (Lane's Battery)
Lloyd's (North Carolina) Battery
Patterson's (Georgia) Battery
Ross' (Georgia) Battery

*Jones' Battalion* [10]
MAJ. H.P. JONES

Morris (Virginia) Artillery, (R.C.M. Page's Battery)
Orange (Virginia) Artillery (Peyton's Battery)
Turner's (Virginia) Battery
Wimbish's (Virginia) Battery

*Nelson's Battalion*
MAJ. WILLIAM NELSON

Amherst (Virginia) Artillery (Kirkpatrick's Battery)
Fluvanna (Virginia) Artillery (Ancell's Battery)
Huckstep's (Virginia) Battery
Johnson's (Virginia) Battery [11]
Milledge (Georgia) Artillery (Milledge's Battery)

[8] Including all batteries mentioned in the reports, or in the reorganization of October 4, and not elsewhere accounted for. Brooke's, Dearing's, and Nelson's Virginia batteries joined after the campaign had terminated.
[9] First Virginia Artillery.
[10] With D.H. Hill's division at Sharpsburg.
[11] Marmaduke Johnson's battery.

*Miscellaneous*

Cutshaw's (Virginia) Battery
Dixie (Virginia) Artillery (Chapman's Battery)
Magruder (Virginia) Artillery (T.J. Page, Jr.'s Battery)
Rice's (Virginia) Battery, Capt. W.H. Rice [12]
Thomas (Virginia) Artillery (E.J. Anderson's Battery) [13]

## CAVALRY
### MAJ. GEN. JAMES E.B. STUART

*Hampton's Brigade*
### BRIG. GEN. WADE HAMPTON

1st North Carolina, Col. L.S. Baker
2d South Carolina, Col. M.C. Butler
10th Virginia
Cobb's (Georgia) Legion, Lieut. Col. P.M.B. Young
Jeff Davis Legion, Lieut. Col. W.T. Martin

*Lee's Brigade*
### BRIG. GEN. FITZ LEE

1st Virginia, Lieut. Col. L. Tiernan Brien
3d Virginia, Lieut. Col. John T. Thornton
4th Virginia, Col. Williams C. Wickham
5th Virginia, Col. T.L. Rosser
9th Virginia

*Robertson's Brigade*
### BRIG. GEN. B.H. ROBERTSON
### COL. THOMAS T. MUNFORD

2d Virginia, Col. T.T. Munford, Lieut. Col. Burks
6th Virginia
7th Virginia, Capt. S.B. Myers
12th Virginia, Col. A.W. Harman
17th Virginia Battalion

[12] Not mentioned between September 1-22, but probably with the army in reserve.
[13] Left at Leesburg.

HORSE ARTILLERY
CAPT. JOHN PELHAM

Chew's (Virginia) Battery
Hart's (South Carolina) Battery
Pelham's (Virginia) Battery

# FURTHER READING

Armstrong, Marion V. "A Failure of Command? A Reassessment of the Generalship of Edwin V. Sumner and the Federal II Corps at the Battle of the Antietam," 67–145, in Steven E. Woodworth, ed., *Leadership and Command in the American Civil War.* Campbell, Cal.: Savas Woodbury Publishers, 1996. This revisionist evaluation of Major General Edvin V. Sumner as a corps commander at Antietam, particularly of his role in the West Woods disaster, is highly recommended to intermediate and advanced students of the battle. The essay's thesis deserves serious consideration because it is based on sound research in the primary sources and is supported by an excellent series of maps.

*Blue & Gray Magazine.* Popular magazines like this one often publish interesting articles on specific aspects of the Antietam campaign. Here are a few examples from this one periodical, among a number in the field: Ted Alexander, "Forgotten Valor: Off the Beaten Path at Antietam," 13, no. 1 (Fall 1995): 8–15,19, 48, 51–64; Paul Chiles, "Artillery Hell: The Guns of Antietam," 16, no. 2 (Holiday 1998): 6–10, 12–16, 24–25, 41, 43–44, 49–58; Dennis E. Frye, "Stonewall Attacks! The Siege of Harpers Ferry," 6, no. 1 (August–September 1987): 8–21, 24–27, 47–54; Jerry W. Holsworth, "Uncommon Valor: Hood's Texas Brigade in the Maryland Campaign," 13, no. 6 (Summer 1996): 6–18, 20, 50–55; Thomas McGrath, "The Corn Exchange Regiment's Baptism of Fire," 16, no. 1 (Fall 1998): 22–26; Timothy J. Reese, "Howell Cobb's Brigade at Crampton's Gap," 15, no. 3 (Winter 1998): 6–21, 47–48, 50–54, 56.

Catton, Bruce. *Mr. Lincoln's Army.* Garden City, N.Y.: Doubleday, 1951. Bruce Catton devoted the second half of this volume of his trilogy on the Army of the Potomac to the Antietam campaign. His engaging style, one of the liveliest among Civil War historians, makes this book a good choice for beginning students of the war.

*Civil War Regiments: A Journal of the American Civil War.* This quarterly periodical published five works on specific aspects of the Maryland campaign in its volume 5, number 3 issue. The wealth of detail here may intimidate beginners, but is highly recommended for experienced students. Each contribution is thoroughly researched and the volume features crisp maps.

Clemens, Tom. "'Black Hats' Off to the Original 'Iron Brigade,'" *Columbiad* 1:1 (Spring 1997), 46–58. A well researched corrective to the myths that the Black Hat Brigade won the nickname "Iron Brigade" at the Battle of South Mountain, and that John Gibbon's command was the only "Iron Brigade."

Dowdey, Clifford and Louis H. Manarin, eds. *The Wartime Papers of Robert E. Lee.* Boston: Little Brown, 1961. A valuable collection of primary documents. Chapter 7 contains twenty-one items from the Maryland campaign, thirteen of them communications from Lee to President Jefferson Davis.

Editors of *Blue & Gray Magazine, Blue and Gray Magazine's History and Tour Guide of the Antietam Battlefield.* Columbus, Ohio: Blue & Gray Enterprises, 1995. In 1985 this popular periodical published two articles that traced out an informative tour of the Antietam battlefield, intended for first-time or somewhat-experienced visitors. This book combines the two publications into one work, in a soft cover format suited to tossing onto your carseat or carrying on a hike.

Frassanito, William A. *Antietam: The Photographic Legacy of America's Bloodiest Day.* New York. Charles Scribners' Sons, 1978. In a sequel to a similar work on Gettysburg, this dramatic book presents a fascinating series of "then" and "now" photographs of the Antietam battlefield and an authoritative history of the haunting images that Alexander Gardner and James F. Gibson took after the combat. Frassanito also offers beginners a good survey history of the battle.

Freeman, Douglas Southall. *R.E. Lee: A Biography.* 4 vols. New York and London: Charles Scribner's Sons, 1934–35. Chapters 25–28 of volume 2 of this magisterial work cover the Sharpsburg campaign. Freeman's reverence for Lee prevented him from writing

an objective biography, but his portrait of this commander is a
towering classic in Civil War literature.

_____. *Lee's Lieutenants: A Study in Command.* 3 vols. New
York: Charles Scribner's Sons, 1942–44. Chapters 8–14 of
volume 2 treat the Maryland campaign. With the entry
above, Lee's Lieutenants remains the finest work done on
the Army of Northern Virginia.

Gallagher, Gary, ed. *Antietam: Essays on the 1862 Maryland
Campaign.* London and Kent, Ohio: Kent State University
Press, 1989. Researchers who are already familiar with the
general history of the Antietam campaign should study this
compilation, a slender volume full of thoughtful analysis.
Four Civil War historians contributed essays to it, based on
the best scholarship available in the late 1980s.

_____. ed. *Lee the Soldier.* Lincoln and London: University of
Nebraska Press, 1996. This useful compilation includes
memoranda of post-war conversations with Robert E. Lee,
which are especially valuable because the general wrote no
memoirs; evaluations of his generalship; short surveys of
his campaigns; and an excellent annotated bibliography. D.
Scott Hartwig, "Robert E. Lee and the Maryland Campaign,"
331–355, is an informative treatment of its subject.

Harsh, Joseph L. *Confederate Tide Rising: Robert E. Lee and
the Making of Southern Strategy, 1861–1862.* Kent, Ohio,
and London: The Kent State University Press, 1998. This
work, important for its fresh interpretations, is required
reading for everyone interested in the background to the
Maryland campaign. Its preface explains that *Confederate
Tide Rising* represents the introductory portion of a larger
manuscript, the remainder to be published later. At the time
that this "Further Reading" section was prepared, the fol-
low-on work had not yet appeared, but Harsh's high level of
scholarship assures that it can be recommended in advance.

Hassler, Warren W., Jr. *General George B. McClellan, Shield of
the Union.* Baton Rouge, Louisiana, Louisiana State
University Press, 1957. Hassler swam against the main cur-

rent of McClellan historiography when he wrote this sympathetic biography of the Young Napoleon.

Johnson, Curt, and Richard C. Anderson, Jr. *Artillery Hell: The Employment of Artillery at Antietam.* College Station, Tex.: Texas A&M University Press, 1995. In 1940 Antietam had no cannon indicating the battlefield's artillery positions. Major Joseph Mills Hanson identified the most important field gun locations, which then were marked by pieces drawn from other national parks. Major Hanson's previously unpublished manuscript, "A Report on the Employment of the Artillery at the Battle of Antietam," forms the centerpiece of this work.

Johnson, Robert Underwood, and Clarence Clough Buel, eds. *Battles and Leaders of the Civil War.* 4 vols. New York: Century Company, 1887. Several articles on the Antietam campaign appear in volume 2 of this important primary source, including ones by George B. McClellan, William B. Franklin, James Longstreet, John G. Walker, and other participants.

Large, George R., and Joe A. Swisher. *Battle of Antietam: The Official History by the Antietam Battlefield Board.* Shippensburg, Pa.: Burd Street Press, 1998. A Congressional act of 1890, expanded in later years, appropriated money for locating, surveying, and preserving the lines of battle at Antietam and other sites of the Maryland campaign. The result of this legislation was the roughly 240 cast-iron tablets erected by the Antietam Battlefield Board, nearly all of which still stand. The Large and Swisher book details the location of each of these markers and makes their text conveniently available.

Luvaas, Jay, and Harold W. Nelson, eds. *The U.S. Army War College Guide to the Battle of Antietam: The Maryland Campaign of 1862.* Carlisle, PA,: South Mountain Press, 1987. This is an extremely useful but advanced guidebook. Students who have mastered the general history of the campaign and battle, and who have taken tours like those in the

*Blue & Gray* articles, will benefit greatly from the Luvaas and Nelson book. It gives clear directions from one point to another at South Mountain, Harpers Ferry and Antietam, and at each stop presents excerpts from the *Official Records*, the after-action reports that describe the fighting at that particular place.

McClellan, George B. *McClellan's Own Story.* New York: C.L. Webster and Company, 1887. Although students must use this posthumous autobiography cautiously, it is nonetheless an essential primary account. For an informative history of this source, researchers should consult "Epilogue: A Memory For History," pp. 403–6 in Stephen Sears biography of McClellan, cited elsewhere in these suggested readings.

Murfin, James V. *The Gleam of Bayonets: The Battle of Antietam and the Maryland Campaign of 1862.* New York and London: Thomas Yoseloff, 1965. With Sears' *Landscape Turned Red*, this work is one of the two best Antietam studies written during the twentieth century. Murfin greatly advanced the study of the Maryland campaign. A strong feature of this book is that it made the 1904 version of the Ezra Carman-E.B. Cope maps of the Battle of Antietam readily available.

Palfrey, Francis W. *The Antietam and Fredericksburg.* New York: Charles Scribner's Sons, 1882. The most important nineteenth-century study of this campaign, and of the Fredericksburg operations that followed it, written by a veteran of the 20th Massachusetts. Palfrey was an 1851 graduate of Harvard and his high-blown prose and unadorned details are daunting to readers of later generations, but serious students of Antietam must eventually come to terms with this somber volume.

Palmer, Michael A. *Lee Moves North: Robert E. Lee on the Offensive.* New York, et al.: John Wiley & Sons, Inc., 1998. Palmer focuses on three operations in which Robert E. Lee pursued the strategic offensive and failed: the Antietam, Gettysburg, and Bristoe campaigns. He argues that each of these cases were characterized by Lee's penchant for quickly planned offensives unsupported by adequate logistics, his secretive approach to dealings with Richmond, his army's poor staff work, and other weaknesses. Palmer contends that Lee did not consider the Maryland campaign (pages 1–37) a failure and did not learn any lessons from it.

Priest, John M. *Antietam: The Soldiers' Battle.* Shippensburg, Pa.: White Mane Press, 1989. Priest's work is too detailed for beginners, but is strongly recommended to those who have already mastered Murfin and Sears. The text gives a harrowing account of the combat, told from the perspective of scores of individual soldiers, and the maps provide a valuable supplement to those in *The Gleam of Bayonets.*

_____. *Antietam: The Soldiers' Battlefield: A Self-Guided Mini-Tour.* Shippensburg, Pa.: White Mane Press, 1994. Priest compiled this guidebook from his Antietam volume, discussed above. Like his narrative works, this is not the best choice for first-time visitors to Antietam, but "veterans" will greatly enjoy it.

_____. *Before Antietam: The Battle for South Mountain.* Shippensburg, Pa.: White Mane Press, 1992. Like the author's Antietam volume, this one is a challenge for new students, but experienced readers will profit from its narrative and maps.

Pryor, Elizabeth Brown. *Clara Barton.* Washington, D.C.: Government Printing Office, 1981. This is the National Park Service's handbook about America's most famous nurse, whose work at Antietam represented a milestone in medical history. The clearly written and well illustrated text offers a fine introduction to its subject.

Reilly, Oliver T. *The Battlefield of Antietam.* Hagerstown, Md.: Hagerstown Bookbinding & Printing Company, 1906. Born five and a half years before September 1862, O.T. Reilly grew up listening to the war stories of Sharpsburg residents and Antietam veterans, and spent decades hiking the battlefield, collecting relics, and giving tours. His souvenir pamphlet, long available through reprint, is a collection of fascinating photographs and anecdotes.

Rowland, Thomas J. *George B. McClellan and Civil War History: In the Shadow of Grant and Sherman.* Kent, Ohio, and London: The Kent State University Press, 1998. Rowland makes an exciting historiographical presentation, which draws on the literature of the 1980s and 1990s to appraise McClellan's generalship more favorably than the traditional assessments of Kenneth P. Williams, Bruce Catton, T. Harry Williams, and others. This book argues that McClellan's reputation suffered because historians subjected his field results in 1862 to an unfair comparison with those of Grant and Sherman in 1864–1865, when Confederate forces were demoralized and much weaker than during the first two years of the war. Rowland considers the Antietam campaign at several points, most closely on pages 216–225.

Schildt, John W., *Drums Along the Antietam.* Parsons, W. Va.: McClain Printing Company, 1972. Every Civil War battlefield should have a local historian as dedicated as John Schildt. He has gathered a wealth of lore about the families, farms, and churches of the Antietam Valley and made it available in this and other books.

Sears, Stephen W. *Landscape Turned Red: The Battle of Antietam.* New Haven and New York: Ticknor & Fields, 1983. This and Murfin's *The Gleam of Bayonets* are the two best Antietam histories of the twentieth-century. *Landscape Turned Red* is based on extensive research in manuscripts and other primary sources. Sears vividly describes the personalities and maneuvers of the campaign and clearly connects one event to another.

_____. *George B. McClellan: The Young Napoleon.* New York: Ticknor & Fields, 1988. This treatment of McClellan's entire life details the flaws in his personality and generalship. Sears' portrait reinforces the conventional assessment of Little Mac.

_____. ed. *The Civil War Papers of George B. McClellan: Selected Correspondence: 1860–1865.* New York: Ticknor & Fields: 1989. Chapters 8 and 9 present the surviving items of McClellan's important correspondence, from the Antietam

campaign through his departure from the Army of the
Potomac.

Stotelmyer, Steven R. *Bivouacs of the Dead.* Baltimore: Toomey
Press, 1992. Visitors to Sharpsburg often wonder what
became of the thousands of corpses left strewn for miles
around the village. This well illustrated book accounts for
what happened to the remains of the soldiers killed at
Antietam and South Mountain. Stotelmyer covers the
Antietam National Cemetery, Washington Confederate
Cemetery (Hagerstown, Maryland), Mount Olivet Cemetery
(Frederick, Maryland), and Elmwood Confederate Cemetery
(Shepherdstown, West Virginia).

Thomas, Emory. *Robert E. Lee.* New York and London: W.W.
Norton, 1995. This extremely well conceived and executed
biography provides an important companion to Freeman's
classic work. Freeman wrote about Lee the general, Thomas
about Lee the man. Chapter twenty treats the Second
Manassas and Sharpsburg campaigns.

Tilberg, Frederick. *Antietam: Antietam National Battlefield,
Maryland.* Washington, D.C.: Government Printing Office,
1960. The National Park Service's handbook for the battlefield, this booklet has become somewhat dated but is still an
excellent introduction to the campaign for first-time visitors
to Antietam and for beginning students.

United States War Department. *The War of Rebellion: A
Compilation of the Official Records of the Union and
Confederate Armies.* 127 vols., index, and atlas.
Washington, D.C.: Government Printing Office 1880–1901.
The fundamental published primary source on the Antietam
campaign. The reports and correspondence of the Maryland
operations are found in series I, volume 19, parts 1 and 2,
and some additional reports in volume 51, part 1. The
Luvaas and Nelson guidebook, cited elsewhere in this list-
ing, makes available in convenient form a collection of
excerpts from this essential source.

Williams, Kenneth P. *Lincoln Finds a General.* 5 vols. New
York: Macmillan, 1949–59. The Antietam campaign is cov-

ered in volume 1, chapter 13, and volume 2, chapter 14, of this survey history of the war which focuses on the Northern high command. Along with works by T. Harry Williams and Bruce Catton, *Lincoln Finds a General* founded the conventional school of McClellan historiography.

# INDEX